P9-DEF-062

The Pastor's Guide *to* Effective Preaching

Billy Graham, Maxie Dunnam, John A. Huffman Jr.,
Eugene Peterson, Haddon W. Robinson, Darius Salter,
William Willimon, Elizabeth R. Achtemeier,
James Earl Massey, Marva J. Dawn,
Jana Childers, David Busic

Beacon Hill Press of Kansas City
Kansas City, Missouri

10 9 8 7 6 5 4 3 2 1

Contents

Introduction

"Preaching is God's own way of converting, redeeming, and changing behavior," wrote Thomas Oden.[1] The preacher who has said yes to God's call knows the incredible privilege and the awesome challenge of this exhilarating, yet humbling task.

As a pastor, your planner—or Palm Pilot—are always schedule packed. Week after week the ministry of preaching vies for substantive hours on the calendar. You are a communicator, a connector—between, on the one hand, the world of the sacred, the Scriptures, the Presence and, on the other hand, the terra firma world of 8-5 schedules, dentist appointments, and soccer practice. To feed your own faith, you meditate in the holy Word and commune with Christ. But then, Sunday is always looming. In a matter of hours you will again mount the pulpit or chancel before your congregation. Your charge will be—*preach*. Communicate, articulate, make plain the message of God in clear, simple words that all persons can easily grasp. Represent the world of the holy and connect with postmodern individuals in the pew.

In preparation, you will immerse yourself in the Scripture passage(s), wrestle with the text, and develop the sermon. In a real sense you will represent not only Christ and the Scriptures, but the church as well. Thomas Long wrote, "The preacher is a member of the community, set apart by them and sent to the scripture to search, to study, and to listen obediently on their behalf. . . . Whatever needs of the church and world have been brought to the text by the preacher, when the claims of God through the scripture are seen and heard, the preacher turns back toward those who wait—and tells the truth."[2] What a call! What an entrustment! What a life! *And who is sufficient for these things?* (2 Cor. 2:16, KJV).

This sacred ministry of preaching is addressed in this book by veteran leaders in the field. *The Pastor's Guide to Effective Preaching* is designed to bring you wisdom, sound thinking, and practical advice for this ministry. The essays cover a range of topics, but in general are compiled around the theme of preaching for the transformation and spiritual formation of the hearers. Included also are articles on the nature of expository preaching, communication issues in preaching, and effective sermon planning. Each author brings his or her distinctive personality, experience, ministry approach, and writing style to this book. When you read the book as a whole, however, you will find a wealth of insights and counsel that will assist you in becoming a more effective pastor/ preacher. These authors represent cumulative years of effective preaching. Allow God to minister to you through their writings. You'll be challenged to be a better minister of the gospel of Christ.

Notes

1. Thomas Oden, *Pastoral Theology: Essentials of Ministry* (New York: Harper-Collins, 1983), 136.

2. Thomas G. Long, *The Witness of Preaching* (Louisville: Westminster/John Knox Press, 1989), 45.

Billy Graham, world-renowned author, preacher, and evangelist, has delivered the gospel message to more people face-to-face than anyone in history. He has ministered on every continent and has had the privilege of knowing heads of state throughout the world. He is the founder and chairman of the Board of Directors of the Billy Graham Evangelistic Association.

Dr. Graham has authored several best-selling books including *Hope for the Troubled Heart, Angels, How to Be Born Again, Peace with God,* and *The Secret of Happiness.* He and his wife, Ruth, reside in the mountains of North Carolina.

1

Evangels of Grace
Billy Graham

THE WELL-KNOWN GERMAN THEOLOGIAN RUDOLPH BULTMANN asked the question that is appropriate for our times, "How do we communicate the gospel in a secularistic and technological age?" This question might be put differently in different cultures, but all of us are concerned with effectively communicating the gospel. In many circumstances, it means what missiologists have called "contextualization." This means we adapt our methods to the culture and society in which we are called to proclaim the gospel. But let's make it clear: we have no authority from Scripture to alter the *message*. The message can never be contextualized.

Thus, I would like to ask this question again: *How do we communicate the gospel with power in this materialistic, scientific, rebellious secular, immoral, humanistic age?*

1. The Key

The key to the basic question that unlocks the door to effective gospel communication is in 1 Cor. 2:2, "For I resolved to know nothing while I was with you except Jesus Christ and him crucified."

Look at the context of this verse. When Paul went to Corinth, it was one of the most idolatrous, pagan, intellectual, and immoral cities in the entire Roman world. If you wanted to condemn someone as an immoral person, you called him a "Corinthian." When Paul looked at this city, and felt God's leadership to start a church there, what did he do? How could he communicate in that place? Do not forget, there was not a single other Christian in town. Paul was the only believer. What would he do? What would you do? How do you "preach the gospel" in an atmosphere alien to its very nature? That is always the question. It is the prime question today.

2. The Power of the Gospel

If we could ask Paul personally those searching questions, perhaps he would say, "My intelligence alone will not be able to handle it. I do not have the logic or the arguments to compel the Corinthians to accept the truth of the gospel." What, then, did he do? He said, with positive faith, "For I resolved to know nothing while I was with you except Jesus Christ and him crucified." Why such a statement? Paul knew that there was a built-in power in the Cross; it has its own communicative power. Paul well knew that the Holy Spirit takes the simple message of the Cross, with its message of redemptive love and grace, through the proclaiming of Christ, and infuses it into lives with authority and power.

Furthermore, the Spirit's work is vital, for "the man without the Spirit does not accept the things that come from the Spirit of God, for they are foolishness to him, and he cannot understand them, because they are spiritually discerned" (1 Cor. 2:14).

Therefore, when we go to proclaim the gospel of Christ, we by faith know that when we proclaim the *kerygma* (as Paul describes it in 1 Cor. 15), when we preach Christ crucified, there's a power—dynamite—in it. Proclaimers of the gospel must *always* realize, as Paul stressed, that the natural man simply cannot accept the truth of Christ unless the veil is lifted by the Holy Spirit.

But the marvelous fact is, the Holy Spirit takes the message and communicates it to the heart and mind, with power, and breaks down every barrier. It's a supernatural act of the Spirit of God. No evangelist can have God's touch on his or her ministry until he or she realizes these realities and preaches in the power of the Holy Spirit. In the final analysis, the Holy Spirit is the Communicator.

3. Some Safe Assumptions

Now, I want to say a word about some important aspects of proclamation of the gospel. Let me be personal right here! When I go out and proclaim the gospel, in every congregation, and any group—whether it's on a street corner in Nairobi; or in a meeting in Seoul, Korea; or in a tribal situation in Zaire; or in a large stadium in New York City—I know there are certain things that are true in the hearts and minds of all people, certain psychological and spiritual factors that exist in everyone. As I begin to communicate, I can trust the Holy Spirit to strike certain responsive chords in every human heart that hears.

    a. Life's needs are not totally met by social improvement or material affluence. This is true around the world and in every culture. Jesus said, "A man's life does not consist in the abundance of his possessions" (Luke 12:15).

    b. There is an essential "emptiness" in every life without Christ. All humanity keeps crying for something, something—they do not know what it is. Give a person a million dollars—it doesn't satisfy. Or give the person sex and every form of sensuality; nor does that ever satisfy the deep longing inside that keeps crying for satisfaction. I talked to a man some time ago who is supposedly one of the sex symbols of America. He said, "I've slept with some of the most beautiful women in the world. But it doesn't bring fulfillment and peace." He went on, "I'm one of the most miserable men in the world." There is another level to life. That we can assume as we preach Christ in the power of the Holy Spirit.

I have spoken at a number of the world's most famous universities, and I have heard the pitiful cry of youth who are intellectually, psychologically, and spiritually lost. They are searching for something, and they don't know what it is. I once talked to Dr. Bok, president of Harvard University. I asked him what was the greatest thing lacking among the students. He thought for a moment and then answered, "Commitment." Pascal put it right when he said, "There's a God-shaped vacuum in every life that only God can fill." When we proclaim the gospel, we're talking directly to that emptiness. The person with whom you're communicating, whether in personal witnessing or before a group, has a built-in receptivity to the message of the Cross, because Christ alone fills the void.

c. *We can assume in our hearers a loneliness.* Some have called it "cosmic loneliness." I have a friend who is a psychiatrist and a theologian at an American university. I asked him on one occasion, "What is the greatest problem of the patients that come to you for help?" He thought a moment and said, "Loneliness." He went on, "When you get right down to it, it is a loneliness for God." We all sense something of that. For example, we can be in a crowd of people, even at a party, and suddenly, with all the people around laughing, a loneliness will sweep over you—just for a moment. That is "cosmic loneliness," and it is everywhere: loneliness in the suburbs, loneliness in the ghettos, loneliness in Africa, loneliness in Latin America, loneliness in Japan. It is a loneliness that only God can fill. You can assume that also in preaching Christ.

d. *We are speaking to people who have a sense of guilt.* This is perhaps the most universal of all human experiences, and it is devastating. The head of a mental institution in London said, "I could release half of my patients if I could but find a way to rid them of their sense of guilt." What a tremendously relevant message we have for that problem. This is what the Cross is all about. When we preach Christ, we are speaking directly to the nagging, depressing problem of guilt. And that problem is always there. You don't make people feel guilty; they already know it. Tell them what the guilt is. Tell them it is rebellion against God, and tell them the Cross is the answer!

   e. There is the universal fear of death. We do not like to talk about death in our generation. But death is real. In many parts of the world you can turn on the television and see movie stars such as Marilyn Monroe or Clark Gable; they look alive, but they are dead. Somehow television, especially in Western society, has cushioned death. Yet the specter is always there. The subtle fear cannot be silenced. But here is the glorious news: our Lord came to nullify death. In His own death and resurrection, He made three things inoperative: sin, death, and hell. That's the message of the Cross.

4. *Some Principles of Communicating the Gospel*

   All these assumptions can be realized as we preach Christ. The Holy Spirit will apply the message to these deep-seated needs. But now the question is: In the midst of all these assumptions, *how* are we to communicate the gospel?

   a. Communicate the gospel with *authority*. Preach it with assurance, remembering that "faith comes from hearing the message, and the message is heard through the word of Christ" (Rom. 10:17). If I have one criticism of modern theological education, especially in Europe and America, it is this: I do not think we are putting enough emphasis on authoritative preaching. Where are the great preachers today? Where are the Luthers, the Calvins, the Knoxes, the Spurgeons? Churches are constantly asking for recommendations for pastors, and they all say, "In our particular situation, we have to have somebody who can preach." But where are the preachers who preach with confidence and authority? When you have a conference, you always see the same names: men who can preach authoritatively. If you want God's best on your ministry, preach with power and authority. But how does one learn to communicate with such power?

   In my early days, when I started to prepare a sermon, I got a book of sermons by a famous Texas preacher. I took two of his sermons, along with a couple of his outlines, and I would preach them out loud 10 to 20 times. In my first sermon, in Bostic, Florida, at the Baptist church, I was trembling. I had prepared four sermons. I practiced as I described, until I knew that each one of them would last 40 minutes. I got up and preached all four in 8 minutes! So don't get discouraged, just keep going—work hard. It takes hard work to prepare effective messages. Saturate yourself in the Word of God. Get to the place where you can say, as

Spurgeon said of Ps. 119, "Oh the depths." Pray and pray until you *know* you have God's message. Seek God until you are sure His divine anointing is on you. Actually, your whole life is a preparation to preach. Then, as Spurgeon said, "Take your text and make a beeline for the cross."

Dr. Sid Bonnell said to his class at Princeton, "If you are preaching under the anointing of the Holy Spirit, the hearers will hear another 'Voice.'" No one is ever preaching until the people are conscious of that other "Voice." Are people conscious of that other "Voice" when you preach? Are you Spirit-filled (Eph. 5:18)? Do you preach with His authority? That is absolutely essential to the communication of the gospel. One reason the people listened to Jesus was that He spoke as one having authority.

Preach with authority. When you quote God's Word, He will use it. He will never allow it to return void.

One day my wife was in the famous London bookstore, Foyles. A fellow came out, discouraged and despondent. He said to my wife, "You look like a real Christian. My family's torn up." He said, "I'm on the verge of suicide." She asked, "Well, why not go out to the Harringay Arena tonight and hear Billy Graham?" "Oh," he said, "I don't think he could help me. I'm beyond help." But she gave him some tickets, and he came. She didn't see him for a year. The next year, when we were at Wembley Stadium, she went back to Foyles. That same little fellow came running out. He said, "Oh, Mrs. Graham, that night I went to Harringay and I was converted to Christ. And I'm the happiest person in Britain!" He went on, "The verse your husband preached on that night that God saved me was a verse from the Psalms, "I am like a pelican of the wilderness: I am like an owl of the desert"(Ps. 102:6, KJV). My wife scratched her head and said, "I never thought of that as a gospel verse." But he said, "That verse described me completely and I was saved." You see, God uses His Word. His power is in the Word.

b. Preach the gospel with *simplicity.* Dr. James S. Stewart, of Edinburgh, said, "You never preach the Gospel unless you preach it with simplicity." He said further, "If you shoot over the heads of your hearers, you don't prove anything except you have a poor aim." We must learn to take the profoundest things of God and proclaim them with simplicity.

In our Berlin Congress on Evangelism in 1966, one of the papers read by an American theologian was deep and involved. Many of the Christians really did not understand what he was talking about. But there was an African there, dressed in his native dress, and he had not been able to make out a thing that the learned professor said. But he went right up and hugged the speaker and kissed him in front of every-body. And he said, "You know, I don't understand a thing you say, but I'm so glad that a man who knows as much as you know is on our side." The sentiment was great, but we must communicate so that people un-derstand as well. Preach it with simplicity.

I have a friend on the West Coast of America. He is in the Meth-odist Church. One Sunday before the worship hour, he decided he was going to present some visual education for the children. He decided he would preach his children's sermon with all sorts of slides he had made during the week. This, he thought, would illustrate his simple sermon and help the children understand. To his amazement he found that the older people began to come early until the church was packed to hear his children's sermons, and the attendance at his eleven o'clock service was dropping. He had made that grand discovery that the more simple he made his communication, the more people came to hear. People want simplicity. I am sure that was one of the secrets of the ministry of our Lord. The Bible says, "The common people heard him gladly" (Mark 12:37, KJV). Why? For one central reason. They understood Him. He spoke their language.

c. Preach with *repetition.* Professor James Denney, of Glasgow, once said that Jesus probably repeated himself more than 500 times. That is an encouragement to every evangelist. The gospel may at times seem "old" to us, but repeat and repeat and repeat it. It is "news" to multi-tudes. Never tire, and never be embarrassed to share the news over and over again.

d. Preach it with *urgency;* preach it for *decision.* People are dying. You may be speaking to some who will hear the gospel for the last time. Preach with the urgency of Christ. Preach it to bring your hearers to Christ. Preach for decision. Preach for a verdict as Jesus did. The call to repentance and faith is part of the proclamation (*kerygma*) too.

e. Never forget, we are to communicate the gospel by a *holy life.* This is essential. Did you know that our world today is looking primarily for men and women of integrity, communicators who back up their min-istry with their lives? Your preaching emerges out of what you are. We *must* be a holy people. Those who have affected me most profoundly have not been the great orators. It is those who have been holy men and women. That is where the stress must be placed. Robert Murray Mc-Cheyne said, "A holy man is an awful weapon in God's hand." Paul said, "I keep under my body, and bring it into subjection" (1 Cor. 9:27, KJV).

We must take that seriously. There are three avenues through which the devil attacks young evangelists (and older preachers too): money, morals, and pride. As ministers of the gospel, you will battle with all three all your life. Be ready. The devil will set traps for you constantly.

When we first started in evangelism, Cliff Barrows and I deter-mined that we were going to incorporate and have a board, and pay our-selves a set salary. It caused a furor. Some said, "You're going to ruin evangelism." But I believe that God has honored the way we've handled the finances. We must never bring reproach on evangelism over money. Evangelists are so vulnerable right there. Be holy!

Nor is a holy life merely negative—"don't do this, or, don't do that." It is positive. You must immerse yourself in the Word of God. You must be a person of prayer. A disciplined devotional life is vital to holy living.

f. We communicate the gospel by our *love of our fellowman.* "All men will know that you are my disciples, if you love one another" (John 13:35). A layperson in Boston went boldly into a hotel, walked up to a lady, and said, "Do you know Christ?" She told her husband about it. Her husband said, "Didn't you tell him to mind his own business?" She replied, "But, my dear, if you'd seen the expression on his face and heard the earnestness with which he spoke, you would have thought it *was* his business."

When you speak to people about Christ, personally or in preach-ing, do they think that it is your business? Do you really love people? Does it show? Do they sense your compassion?

One of our associate evangelists was preaching in Central America at the university on one occasion. He tried to win the students to Christ, and they showed him a great deal of hostility. One student was especially hostile. After the service, this girl came up to him (she was working on her doctorate degree), and she said, "I don't believe any of that hogwash." He said, "Well, I don't think I agree; but do you mind if I pray for you?" She said, "No one ever prayed for me before. I don't guess it will do any harm." He bowed his head, but she looked straight ahead and was defiant when he started to pray. As he prayed for the conversion of that girl, the tears began to flow down his cheeks. When he opened his eyes, she was broken up with tears and said, "No one in my whole life has loved me enough to shed a tear for me." They sat down on a bench and that girl accepted the Lord as her Savior. How many of us have loved so much that we have shed tears?

g. We communicate the gospel by a compassionate *social concern.* This is implied in the love we are to show to others. You may ask, "Billy, do you believe in the social gospel?" Of course I do. I believe that there is a social involvement incumbent and commanded in the Scripture. Look at our Lord. He touched the leper. Can you imagine what that touch meant to that leper, ostracized forever, until his death, who had to cry constantly, "Unclean! Unclean!" Yet, Jesus touched him. Jesus was teaching by example as well as by precept that we have a responsibility to the oppressed, the sick, the poor (Luke 4:18-19). When I think of the starving millions, I can hardly eat my food. This year alone, in Ethiopia, 100,000 people will die of thirst—not hunger—just thirst. They can't get even water, let alone food. And that's only one part of the world.

I was told by one of our economic experts, "We're one crop away from a massive world famine that will affect even the United States." The world is headed toward a gigantic crisis of food. Are we concerned? Our association sends thousands of dollars each year to help. Yes, I believe in a "social gospel." I love people. We are to have a compassionate social concern.

Furthermore, I am not going to apologize for the accusation that Evangelicals throughout the world have done little or nothing in this area. We all have to admit that many of us have not done our share— we have not done enough. It is also wrong to condemn all Evangelicals as having little or no social concern. We have only to think of historical figures like John Wesley, Charles Finney, William Booth, Jonathan Blanchard (the founder of Wheaton College, which has been called the "Harvard" of evangelical education), or Martin Luther King (who came from an evangelical background). We must admit though, that we have not done nearly enough. We have too often been silent in the face of critical social issues.

For two or three generations, when the so-called fundamentalist-modernist controversy was raging in the early 1920s, the reaction by certain groups (even foreign missionary organizations) against the so-called social gospel became so great that they pulled into a shell and gave the Evangelical movement a bad reputation concerning social involvement. For the past few years, a drastic change has been taking place; and there are fine Evangelicals in many parts of the world in the forefront of social change. Go to Nigeria, for example. Four thousand schools have been established there by people who are motivated by the gospel of Jesus Christ.

But never forget, the church goes into the world with an extra dimension in its social concern. We go in the name of our Lord Jesus Christ. We reach out to meet needs and give, but we must always say, "Given in the name of our Lord Jesus Christ." That is our motivation.

And we can often use that means as a vehicle that they can see Christ in us. Therefore, it never becomes mere humanitarianism. We give because God gave.

When I met the former prime minister of Britain, Harold Wilson, he shook hands with me and said, "Oh, yes, we come by your way." I knew what he meant. Keir Hardie helped found the British Labour Party. He had been profoundly influenced by the ministry of evangelist Dwight L. Moody. Keir Hardie was an evangelist all his life, as well as having been deeply involved in helping and organizing the working poor. He founded the British Labour Party because of his social concern, out of love for Christ. And Prime Minister Wilson was a member of that British Labour Party.

When Martin Luther King accepted his Nobel Peace Prize in Stockholm, they asked him, "Where do you get your motivation?" He said, "From my father's evangelistic preaching."

h. We communicate the gospel by our *unity in the Spirit*. How vital it is to realize that if we can stay unified, yet also realize that there is diversity in unity, we can turn the world upside down for Christ. We have the instruments in our hands right now to evangelize the world before the end of this century. For the first time in the history of the Christian Church, the possibility of fulfilling the Great Commission is in our grasp. What an hour! But we must all work together in the "unity of the Spirit through the bond of peace" (Eph. 4:3). This is our task, and this is our job.

Maxie Dunnam, D.D., became president of Asbury Theological Seminary in 1994. Before coming to Asbury he served 12 fruitful years as senior minister at the 6,000-member Christ United Methodist Church in Memphis, Tennessee. From 1975 to 1982 he was world editor of *The Upper Room* daily devotional guide, and prior to that he was Director of Prayer Life and Fellowship for The Upper Room.

Dr. Dunnam holds a bachelor's degree from the University of Southern Mississippi, a master's degree in theology from Emory University, and a doctor of divinity degree from Asbury Theological Seminary. He served recently as one of the presidents of the World Methodist Council and currently chairs the World Evangelism Committee. He is also an elected member of the University Senate of The United Methodist Church and serves on the executive committee of The Association of Theological Schools.

A prolific writer, Dr. Dunnam has authored more than 30 books, including the widely used *Workbook on Living Prayer, This Is Christianity, Unless We Pray,* and two volumes in the Communicator's Commentary series.

Dr. Dunnam and his wife, Jerry, have three adult children: Kim, Kerry, and Kevin.

2
The Personal Holiness
of the Messenger
Maxie Dunnam

"THE GREATEST NEED OF MY CONGREGATION IS MY OWN PERSONAL holiness." I found this challenge from Robert Murray McCheyne true through the years of my pastoral ministry.

I remember a time in my early years of pastoring when I was confronted with this shocking fact: *I am as holy as I want to be.* I was the organizing pastor of a congregation that was experiencing amazing growth. Through this rapid expansion I gave the church my best. I found myself in disagreement with a number of the congregants on an issue of vital concern. Soon the pressure, stress, and tension wore me out. I was physically, emotionally, and spiritually exhausted. I even had thoughts about giving up the ministry. My resources were no longer adequate. Then, one of those God things happened.

I went to a week-long retreat conference led by the world-famous missionary evangelist E. Stanley Jones. I stepped forward to the altar one evening to have the evangelist pray for me. He knew my story. I had shared it with him during the week. As I knelt, he asked me the probing question: "Do you want to be whole? Do you want to be holy?"

That was a sanctifying experience in my life. It changed forever the direction of my ministry. Through the years I have continually asked myself: Do I want to be holy? I have over and again responded that I am as holy as I want to be.

Spiritual, emotional, and relational growth require time and energy —and discipline. Growth in our inner lives diverts us from "pastoral duties" that will eat us alive if we don't keep perspective. When we start in ministry, we're enthusiastic for God and we want nothing more than to be sterling men and women of God. But often early on, for any of several reasons, we're tempted to become preoccupied with success. We start climbing the ladder, looking for a bigger church, a bigger salary, and greater recognition.

Later in ministry we realize how we've strayed. We are aware that we have not ignored spiritual growth and character completely, but we have not had the time or the inclination to concern ourselves with it. Somewhere along the journey some of us wake up to the fact that we have not kept perspective. If we have not forsaken our first love, we have not kept it alive. We've not given it first place. Unfortunately, many of us are in our 40s and 50s before we come to this realization.

I offer this first assertion: *All the permanent fruit and progress that result from our leadership are based on strong character.* Who we are is more important than what we do. This truth is one reason McCheyne's counsel is so important. "The greatest need of my congregation is my own personal holiness."

Our enemy will not leave that unchallenged. And the shocking fact is that *our ministry possesses the potential of handicapping character.* The average parishioner thinks being a pastor makes it easier to grow character. We know otherwise. Vocational ministry can dry and stiffen the earth of the human spirit for several reasons. Consider some.

We have the need for *job security.* How much of the tone and direction of our ministry is shaped by this need? Congregations can be fickle. Staff/parish relations committees can be unrealistic and demanding. Too many churches demand far more of their leader than is possible.

Without conscious awareness, this need for job security affects how we do ministry. The prophetic edge of our ministry is undoubtedly at times impacted by this yawning need. On one occasion early in my ministry I had taken a clear stand on a significant issue that brought me into direct conflict with a number of people in the church. The leaders at one point held a special board meeting to confront the issue—some supporting me and others opposing me.

After the meeting had progressed for some time, one opponent who wielded substantial power in the church asked, "Well, Maxie, what can we expect of you in the future?"

As I reached for an answer, I sensed the Spirit working in me. I heard myself saying, "You can expect me to be consistent with what I feel the gospel is calling me to do."

I wish I could claim that I have always been that clear in my convictions, and always that strong. That simply has not been the case. All of us when we are honest probably would confess that our need for job security has shaped our ministries. And we realize that at times this need has handicapped character building.

Closely related to this need is a second reality—the *frequent moves* of pastors from one congregation to another. When we are moving every two, three, or four years, we don't have the opportunity to clarify troubling issues or work through recurring problems in our own personhood and character.

Another challenge to the development of character and personal holiness is *high and unrealistic expectations*. A woman approached the great Scots preacher Alexander Whyte, complimented him profusely, and said, "Oh, Dr. Whyte, if I could just be as saintly as you are!"

"Madam," he replied, "if you could see into my heart, you would spit in my face."

We may fear that if people discover who we really are, they would lose confidence in us and that our credibility and influence would wane. The human reflex is to hide, put on a mask. Hypocrisy is the greatest temptation of religious professionals.

Another hindrance, the opposite of high expectations, is *stereotyping*. Some people don't want us to be real saints. They don't want us to be people who by word and deed call people to more Christlike behavior. They want us to be merely nice, fulfilling our role with reasonable skill and efficiency. Under this expectation it is easy to become complacent. Instead of striving to become all Christ calls us to be, we simply do what is expected of us: regular hospital calls, decent sermons, warm blessings at women's groups. Ministry may certainly be that much—but it is not only that much—it is far more.

Family pressures present another challenge that can handicap character and can play a significant role in our quest for holiness. These pressures aren't unique to a minister's family, but they are exacerbated by the pressures of ministry. We must pay close attention to our families and how we grow in relation to each other within the family.

As ministers we can deal with the temptations that come with our vocation by continually asking ourselves questions like these:

1. Am I resisting image-building by living as transparently as possible?
2. Am I dealing with the self-deceit that comes from the applause of others?
3. Am I keeping my calling clear, resisting both the temptation for security and a competitive spirit?
4. Am I defensive when asked questions about the use of my time and the consistency of my spiritual disciplines?
5. Am I blaming others for things that are my own fault and the result of my own choices?

"All the permanent fruit and progress that result from our leadership are based on strong character." It is not enough to recognize this truth. We must practice the disciplines that build character and make us the prophet-priests God calls us to be.

A friend in ministry who pastors one of the great churches of our country shared an experience. When he went off to college, he was a candidate for the ministry under the care of a presbytery. Every year he had to appear before this body to give an account of his progress, his plans, and his studies. As he pondered those encounters in retrospect he said, "There's only one thing I remember about those appearances. Mr. Knox, an older white-haired minister, would get up and ask the same question every time I was there. 'Frank, are you making any progress in your walk with Christ?'"

That's a question of spiritual challenge for us to ask ourselves. We probably should get at this question more clearly by asking ourselves three different questions:

1. Am I growing?
2. Do I want to change?
3. How deep is my desire for holiness?

All of us can recall crucial times and events in our ministries that were watershed occasions—times of transition, times that marked dramatic redirection or paradigm shifts in our understanding of vocation, the Christian life, and spirituality. One of those times came for me when I was invited to join the staff of the Upper Room to direct a ministry. My assignment was primarily calling people to a life of prayer, providing direction and resources for growth in the practice of prayer—giving structure to a united expression of prayer by people around the world.

This responsibility forced me to be more deliberate and disciplined in my personal life of prayer, and it introduced me to a wider dimension of spirituality than I had known. During those days I knew no one within the Protestant tradition who was talking about *spiritual formation.* The Roman Catholics have known the importance of this aspect of Christian growth and have used "formation" language through the centuries. Soon we at the Upper Room were talking about spiritual formation and seeking to provide resources for a broader expression of spirituality than we had known before.

I became intensely interested in the great devotional classics. The Upper Room had published a collection of little booklets—selections from the great spiritual writings of the ages—writers whose names I barely knew and whose writings I had not perused: Julian of Norwich, William Law, François Fénelon, Francis of Assisi, Evelyn Underhill, Brother Lawrence, and an array of others. I began keeping company with the saints. I immersed myself in their writings that had endured the centuries and become classic resources for the Christian pilgrimage.

As I absorbed the writings of these saints, I observed some characteristics they had in common:

1. They passionately sought the Lord.
2. They discovered a gracious God.
3. They took Scripture seriously.
4. Jesus was alive in their experience.
5. They practiced discipline, at the heart of which was prayer.
6. They didn't seek ecstasy but surrender of their will to the Lord.
7. They were thirsty for holiness.
8. They lived not for themselves but for God and others.
9. They knew joy and peace, transcending all circumstances.

I submit these characteristics to you as the dynamic that will enable you to stay alive in your ministry and guarantee that you will finish well. I want to elaborate on four of them.

1. The saints practiced discipline that had prayer as its heart

Sister Marie Bonaventura was living a relaxed life as a nun in Rome. After much encouragement, she was persuaded to attend a conference on the Exercises, the disciplines of the spiritual life. The very first meditation was on the purpose and end of humanity. The meditation inspired great fervor in her heart. The priest had scarcely finished speaking when Marie called him to her and said, "Father, I mean to be a saint, and quickly." She then went to her cell, and writing the same words on a scrap of paper, fastened it to her crucifix where it would be a constant reminder.

The saints have all known that there is no way "to be a saint, and quickly." Francis de Sales gave direction for our beginning journey:

> We must begin with a strong and constant resolution to give ourselves wholly to God, professing to Him, in a tender, loving manner, from the bottom of our hearts, that we intend to be His without any reserve, and then we must often go back and renew this same resolution.[1]

Discipline is a challenge to would-be Christians. The Gospels make clear that Jesus' call is to a "narrow way." He couldn't have made it clearer:

Then Jesus told his disciples, "If any want to become my followers, let them deny themselves and take up their cross and follow me. For those who want to save their life will lose it, and those who lose their life for my sake will find it. For what will it profit them if they gain the whole world but forfeit their life? Or what will they give in return for their life?" (*Matt. 16:24-26*, NRSV).

Paul also spoke clearly: "I appeal to you therefore, brothers and sisters, by the mercies of God, to present your bodies as a living sacrifice, holy and acceptable to God, which is your spiritual worship" (Rom. 12:1, NRSV).

I know of no Christian in all the ages that we turn to for teaching and inspiration who did not give himself or herself consistently to discipline and devotion. Disciplines for the spiritual life are at the heart of living out the gospel. The purpose of discipline is to enhance our relationship with Christ, to cultivate a vivid companionship with Him. Through spiritual discipline, we learn to be like Him and live as He lived.

In his book *The Road Less Traveled*, psychiatrist Scott Peck observed:

There are many people I know who possess a vision of [personal] evolution yet seem to lack the will for it. They want, and believe it is possible, to skip over the discipline, to find an easy shortcut to sainthood. Often they attempt to attain it by simply imitating the superficialities of saints, retiring to the desert or taking up carpentry. Some even believe that by such imitation they have really become saints and prophets, and are unable to acknowledge that they are still children and face the painful fact that they must start at the beginning and go through the middle.[2]

Sister Marie Bonoventura's commitment may have been genuine: "Father, I mean to be a saint"—but her timeline—"and quickly"—is really laughable. We "must start at the beginning and go through the middle." The beginning is, as de Sales said, "a strong and constant resolution to give ourselves wholly to God" and the *middle* often consists of going back to renew this same resolution.

2. The saints were concerned about obedience

They were convinced that obedience was essential for their life and growth. Jesus said, "Not everyone who says to me, 'Lord, Lord,' will enter the kingdom of heaven, but only the one who does the will of my Father in heaven. On that day many will say to me, 'Lord, Lord, did we not prophesy in your name, and cast out demons in your name, and do many deeds of power in your name?' Then I will declare to them, 'I never knew you; go away from me, you evildoers'" (Matt. 7:21-23, NRSV).

We do have a right to ask, to seek, and to know the will of God, but once we know it, nothing but obedience will do. The saints sought to arrive at the place in their relationship to Christ that their one longing was to live and walk in a way that would please God and bring glory to His name.

Obedience meant abandonment. Jean-Pierre de Caussade wrote to one who depended upon his spiritual guidance that abandonment to God

> "is, of all practices, the most divine." Your way of acting in times of trouble and distress gives me great pleasure. To be submissive, to abandon yourself entirely without reserve, to be content with being discontented for as long as God wills or permits, will make you advance more in one day than you would in a hundred days spent in sweetness and consolation. Your total abandonment to God, practiced in a spirit of confidence, and of union with Jesus Christ doing always the will of his father, is of all practices, the most divine.[3]

What a simple, yet profound expression of abandonment: "to be content with being discontented for as long as God wills or permits." A pastor friend of mine tells about a member of his congregation who wrote him a letter in the wee hours of the morning. She was troubled and couldn't sleep, so she poured out her feelings on paper. She wrote:

> Which state of grief is this? Or is it grief at all? Just when I experience a little consistency in my new life alone, the next rug I step on is pulled out from under me. Is this all a part of adjusting, or am I being humbled for some greater purpose? My faith is not strong enough to stand on. But my instinct to survive this lonely stretch of my life is so compelling that I'm able to leave the security of my past and go on. Why do my thoughts wake me up in the night, screaming out for paper and pen? There are so few answers, I've found. It would be nice to have the comfort back but not at the expense of my very own soul. So what can I do? Well, I think I will continue to feel my way back through the dark, feeding my faith until someday the lights come on again.[4]

Our spiritual formation is a dynamic process, a growing willingness, or even a willingness to be made willing, to say yes to God every day in every way possible—no matter what the circumstances may be. The more we pay attention to God, the more aware we will become of the yet-to-be redeemed areas of our lives—and the more we will need to abandon ourselves to the transforming power of the indwelling Christ.

Jesus made clear how essential abandonment is when He taught us to pray, "Thy will be done." There are two common ways we pray this prayer. Sometimes we wrestle *against* God. We receive intimations of something God wants us to do, some call—and we wrestle against God because we are not sure we want to respond. Or, we come face-to-face with an issue of God's justice and holiness—and we resist. We don't want to do it.

But there is another kind of wrestling. It is not wrestling against God; here we wrestle *with* God against what opposes God's will. We are engaged in spiritual warfare. We sense that there are forces within our world that are opposed to God's will: sickness, hate, meanness, narrowness of spirit, fear, lethargy, prejudice, and ill will. Understanding that we are up against the forces of darkness, we wrestle against Satan himself. From deep in our inner being we cry, "God's will be done on earth as it is in heaven."

In our spiritual formation, we face the issue of abandonment. Sometimes when we pray, "Thy will be done," we declare that we do not know what is best, but we want God's will. We struggle, we wrestle, we stay in the presence of the Lord until our hearts are made tender and we are ready to trust with surrender God's will.

My favorite story about Lourdes is of an old priest at that famous center who was asked one time by a newspaper reporter to describe the most impressive miracle he'd ever seen there. The reporter expected him to talk about the amazing recovery of someone who had come to Lourdes ill and walked away well. "Not at all," the old priest said. "If you want to know the greatest miracle I have ever seen at Lourdes, it is the look of radiant resignation on the face of those who turn away unhealed!" That's abandonment! That is the expression "Thy will be done" as a declaration of submission, confessing that all we want is God's will—because we know His will is best for us.

Three seeds planted in the soil of obedience will produce the fruit of God's will in our lives: (1) Scripture study; (2) conferencing, that is deliberate and honest sharing with godly persons for edification and discernment of God's will; and (3) divine conviction wrought by the Holy Spirit.

In the divine school of obedience, there is only one textbook—the holy Scripture. The Lord Jesus is, of course, the only model. Those who have walked with Christ for some time have experienced the Holy Spirit's planting of a deep conviction calling us to go a particular direction.

Christian conferencing is another resource for discerning and testing the will of God. We often pay too little attention to this means. Jesus promised that where two or three are gathered in His name, He is present with them. Conferencing with godly persons who love Jesus and who want God's will for their lives and for ours is a helpful and dependable way to seek God's will.

One of the most dramatic moves in my life was based on my accepting God's will through Christian conferencing. My primary calling is clear: to be a pastor/preacher. I was exercising this vocation with great joy, deep meaning, fruitful response, and spiritual growth as senior minister of a large congregation. People were being converted, healed, and coming to maturity in Christ. Our outreach ministries to the "least of these" and to non-Christians were expanding. My wife and I had served that congregation for 12 years and could not have been happier. We intended to stay until retirement.

Then came the call to the presidency of Asbury Theological Seminary. For months I would not even consider the possibility, and I refused to even talk with the search committee. The Holy Spirit impressed upon my wife the notion that I should at least consider what seemed to be a clear call through the committee. I did consider but had no clear direction. In my search for God's will, I began a conferencing process with godly persons I loved and trusted. Some of them had shared my Christian walk for 25 years. I knew they loved God, loved me, and wanted God's best for me.

Through these faithful fellow travelers, I discerned God's will. Since making the decision to accept the seminary presidency, I've had little doubt (and that only during brief periods) that I was in the center of God's will. Over and again my calling to this ministry has been confirmed.

We understand that there is a "general will" of God for all His children that can to a marked degree be ascertained from the Bible. But beyond this general will God has a special application of His will for each individual. The Holy Spirit brings to us the awareness of God's specific will for us. The Scriptures and Christian conferencing are channels He uses to affirm to us God's will for our lives. Once we know His will, nothing but obedience will do.

3. The saints did not seek ecstasy but surrender to the will of the Lord

In her strange and beautiful book *The Cloister Walk*, Kathleen Norris shares her experience of becoming a Benedictine oblate. An oblation is an abbreviated yet powerful profession of monastic vows. A person attaches himself or herself to a particular monastery by signing a document on the altar during mass. The promise is that you will follow the rule of Saint Benedict insofar as your situation in life will allow.

Kathleen said she knew two things: (1) she didn't feel ready to do it, but she had to act, to take the plunge; and (2) she had no idea where it would lead. She confessed,

> The fact that I had been raised a thorough Protestant, with little knowledge of religious orders, and no sense of monasticism as a living tradition, was less an obstacle to my becoming an oblate than the many doubts about the Christian religion that had been with me since my teens. Still, although I had little sense of where I had been, I knew that standing before the altar in a monastery chapel was a remarkable place for me to be, and making an oblation was a remarkable, if not incomprehensible, thing for me to be doing.
>
> The word "oblate" is from the Latin for "to offer." And Jesus Himself is often referred to as an "oblation" in the literature of the early church. Many people now translate "oblate" as "associate," and while that may seem to describe the relationship modern oblates have with monastic communities, it does not adequately convey the religious dimension of being an oblate. Substituting the word "associate" for the "oblation" in reference to Jesus demonstrates this all too well; no longer an offering, Jesus becomes a junior partner in a law firm. The ancient word "oblate" proved instructive for me. Having no idea what it meant, I appreciated its rich history when I first looked it up in the dictionary. But I also felt it presumptuous to claim to be an "offering" and was extremely reluctant to apply to myself a word that had so often been applied to Jesus Christ.[5]

After making that confession, Norris told about the monk who was to be her oblate director, the one who guided her studies of the rule. That period was supposed to last a year but rambled on for nearly three. She expressed gratefulness for this guide who waited patiently for her to sort out her muddle. Finally, she said to him, "I can't imagine why God would want me, of all people, as an offering. But if God is foolish enough to take me as I am, I guess I had better do it."

The monk smiled broadly and said, "You're ready."[6]

That kind of submission was the ongoing concern of the saints. They did not seek ecstasy but surrender to the Lord. They knew that *submission* in the Bible is a *love* word, not a *control* word. It means letting another love you, teach you, influence you, shape you. On the human level, the degree to which we submit to another is the degree to which we will experience that person's love. Regardless of how much love another has for us, it can't be appropriated unless we are open, vulnerable, and submissive.

The saints experienced the same thing in relation to God. They knew it is only when we surrender to the God of grace that we put ourselves in a position for the Spirit to work in us.

In the Scriptures, consider what God did through the apostle Paul as he surrendered to God's direction.

> They went through the region of Phrygia and Galatia, having been forbidden by the Holy Spirit to speak the word in Asia. When they had come opposite Mysia, they attempted to go into Bithynia, but the Spirit of Jesus did not allow them; so, passing by Mysia, they went down to Troas. During the night Paul had a vision: there stood a man of Macedonia pleading with him and saying, "Come over to Macedonia and help us." When he had seen the vision, we immediately tried to cross over to Macedonia, being convinced that God had called us to proclaim the good news to them (_Acts 16:6-10_, NRSV).

Paul was not seeking an ecstatic experience, but he was open and responsive to the Spirit's working in his life. In this instance, it is interesting that he followed what some would label an _ecstatic_ vision. Paul interpreted this vision as God's call to go to Macedonia and preach the gospel.

He went specifically to Philippi, the major city in the Macedonian region, a port city, and easy to get to. Miraculous things happened there. Lydia, a Gentile businesswoman, was converted and the Philippian church was established in her house. A slave girl was delivered from "a spirit of divination," which led to the beating and incarcerating of Paul and Silas. In the jail the third miracle took place. When Paul and Silas were praying and praising God at midnight, God honored their trust and faithfulness by throwing open the prison doors and freeing them. This miracle led to the conversion of the jailer.

These spiritual victories were all the result of Paul's surrender to the Spirit's direction. In this instance, God chose to work through an ecstatic vision. But Paul's openness to the Spirit, his trust in God and not his own wisdom, power, or accomplishments made him an available channel for divine operation. The lesson to us is clear.

Jean-Pierre de Caussade spoke of surrender in these terms:

> Those who have gauged the depths of their own nothingness

can no longer retain any kind of confidence in themselves, nor trust in any way to their works in which they can discover nothing but misery, self-love and corruption. This absolute distrust and complete disregard of self is the source from which alone flow those delightful consolations of souls wholly abandoned to God, and form their unalterable peace, holy joy and immovable confidence in God only.[7]

4. The saints were thirsty for holiness

The Scriptures make a clear distinction between the "children of light" and "children of darkness" (see 1 Thess. 5:4-11). Christ is looking not for admirers but for disciples—those who will conform their lives to His.

Meister Eckhart warned that "there are many who are willing to follow our Lord half-way—but not the other half."[8]

In his introduction to a short collection of passages from *The Imitation of Christ*, Douglas Steere wrote:

> *The Imitation* not only recruits disciples from those who have been admirers. It would train and draw these disciples along until they were willing to enter "the other half," the half where the easy charts and pocket maps vanish and where there are no return tickets available. It, too, would launch them out upon the 70,000 fathoms of water where the foot can no longer touch bottom, where there is no longer any trusting God and keeping your powder dry, but where one must now trust God and take what comes a day at a time.[9]

The end toward which we move in our thirst for holiness is purity of heart. The Puritan divines labeled this *heart-work*. John Flavel, a 17th-century English Puritan, said the "greatest difficulty in conversion, is to *win* the heart to God; the greatest difficulty after conversion, is to keep the heart *with* God. . . . Heart-work is hard work indeed."[10]

The crux of our heart-work toward holiness is our will fully surrendered to Christ so that God can take full possession of us. The apostle Paul expressed it autobiographically: "I have been crucified with Christ; and it is no longer I who live, but it is Christ who lives in me. And the life I now live in the flesh I live by faith in the Son of God, who loved me and gave himself for me" (Gal. 2:19-20, NRSV).

I have a young friend, Tammy, who is living this Christ life dramatically. She was converted at the University of Georgia. She arrived at Asbury Theological Seminary about the time I became president. When she came to the campus, she had only enough money to take her through the first semester. She worked as much as she could, but there was no way she could work enough to pay her tuition and living expenses. So she prayed and exercised her faith. She never asked for money, but time and again when she had no money it would come.

The summer before her last year in seminary, she went to India on a short-term mission. Through a series of circumstances and by following God's call, she returned to India a year later to establish "Grace House," a home for street children. When I last heard from Tammy, there were 60 children under her care in two different facilities. The story is the same as it had been during her years in seminary. She is totally dependent on the Lord.

She sends E-mails to a number of her friends, telling the story of God's miracles. She confesses her dependence on the Lord and her willingness to live sacrificially in order to fulfill God's call on her life.

In an E-mail dated October 4, 2000, she wrote:

> I encourage you to let God take you deeper in prayer and intimacy. I know these are the "Christian catch phrases" these days. But . . . well . . . it's the truth. I guess my prayer for you is that you would go deeper with Jesus, that you would let Him wash through you like a rushing river, cleansing, soothing, filling you in every good way. Intimacy . . . just more of Jesus. That place where you utter a prayer and in an instant, you know it has been answered. That place where you are convicted of your self and sin and in the same moment, encouraged and refreshed. That place in your heart where man's words cannot reach, but one word from God, and you melt.

The thirst for holiness expressed through full surrender opens life to the transforming work of God.

Notes

1. St. Francis de Sales, *A Year with the Saints*, 2.

2. Scott Peck, *The Road Less Traveled* (New York: Simon and Schuster, 1978).

3. Robert Llewelyn, *Joy of the Saints: Spiritual Readings Throughout the Year* (Springfield, Ill.: Templegate Publishers, 1989), 101.

4. "Living Down in the Valley," sermon preached by Norman Neaves, The Church of the Servant, Oklahoma City, Okla., December 2, 1990.

5. Kathleen Norris, *The Cloister Walk* (New York: Riverhead Books, 1996), xvii-xviii.

6. Ibid.

7. Llewelyn, *Joy of the Saints*, 249.

8. Douglas V. Steere, ed., *The Imitation of Christ*, in Great Devotional Classics (Nashville: Upper Room, 1950), 8.

9. Ibid., 8-9.

10. John Flavel, *Keeping the Heart* (Grand Rapids: Sovereign Grace Publishers, 1971), 5, 12.

This chapter is an adapted version of "Taking Risks Without Losing Your Soul" in *Taking Risks in Ministry* in the Beeson Pastoral Series, Dale Galloway, ed. (Kansas City: Beacon Hill Press of Kansas City, 2002), 123-44.

John A. Huffman Jr., D.Min., since 1978 has been the senior minister of St. Andrew's Presbyterian Church in Newport Beach, California.

Dr. Huffman holds a B.A. from Wheaton College, an M.Div. degree from Princeton Theological Seminary, an M.A. from the University of Tulsa, and a D.Min. from Princeton Theological Seminary. Prior to his ministry in California he pastored the Key Biscayne Presbyterian Church in Miami, Florida, and the historic Presbyterian Church in Pittsburgh, Pennsylvania.

He is the author of several books including *Who's In Charge Here? Foundations of Faith from Romans 1-8; Wholly Living—A Study of Philippians; Forgive Us Our Prayers; Liberating Limits—A Fresh Look at the Ten Commandments; Growing Towards Wholeness;* and *Becoming a Whole Family.* He is also the author of the *Joshua* volume of *Communicator's Bible Commentary.* His most recent book is *The Family You Want.*

Each week approximately 5,000 of Dr. Huffman's printed sermons are mailed to all 50 states and over 30 foreign countries. He serves on the board of directors of Gordon-Conwell Theological Seminary, Christianity Today, Int'l, and World Vision, U.S., of which he has been chairman.

He is married to Anne Ridgeway Mortenson, a practicing psychoanalyst, and they have three daughters: Suzanne (deceased), Carla, and Janet.

3

The Role of Preaching in Ministry

John A. Huffman Jr.

PREACHING IS FRONT AND CENTER FOR THOSE OF US CALLED into the pastorate who have as part of our position descriptions the regular teaching and preaching of the Word of God. There are those who would depreciate the role of preaching, arguing for their own particular area of expertise: worship, pastoral care, administration, education, missions, and church growth. All of these are of vital importance in the life of a church. There is a place for persons who devote their whole professional lives to the study and practice of each of these. Not every ordained minister is called to have preaching as his or her foremost specialty.

However, I would encourage you as a pastor never to minimize the importance of preaching and your role as a preacher in your total ministry as a leader in Christ's church. During the past 40 years I have been approached by numerous pastoral nominating committees asking my guidance toward potential candidates. My first question is: "What are you looking for as the number one qualification in a prospective pastor?" In every case they have listed preaching as the highest priority. They are quick to qualify this statement, noting that these other areas are important. The strong presupposition they convey is that churches are intent on calling pastors that they perceive concentrate on the ministry of preaching. This central focus on preaching in ministry does not minimize and can actually enhance the way the rest of the ministries are carried out.

Preaching, for example, is not the same as individual, in-depth psychotherapy. However, healthy preaching provides a superb environment for pastoral care. The best preachers will realize that significant pastoral care is carried out through sensitive, honest, vulnerable, self-disclosing preaching. Harry Emerson Fosdick was one of the first to articulate that pastoral counseling was one of his objectives in the pulpit.

Healthy preaching encourages worship, pastoral care, administration, education, music, missions, and church growth. It provides an environment in the life of a faith community where all of these important ministries happen. Preachers are called to proclaim a holistic gospel that incorporates each of these areas. The degree to which they do this will substantially influence the extent to which the people of God will be able to grow toward wholeness in each of these areas, both within the specific context of worship and in the environments of these specialized ministries.

The major issue is encapsulated in the word *congruence*. In the proclamation of the preached word, biblical themes derive a contemporary authenticity. Week in and week out, faithful preaching—as nowhere else—brings together all of these other dimensions in a way that both builds up individual believers and strengthens the corporate community of faith. Faithful, biblical preaching, sooner or later, addresses all of these topics and many more. How they will fit together in the church will be greatly determined by how they have been handled in the preaching moment.

Church history reveals an ongoing dialogue of human persons with the Word of God as revealed in the Bible. This is a continuous struggle to define biblical authority and to establish ground rules for the meaningful communication of that truth. Central to this struggle is the interplay of pastoral authority and the authority of the Bible. The preached word blends through a hermeneutical process the objective, written word with all of the intellectual, spiritual, social, physical, and psychological resources the preacher's selfhood brings to that process.

One who takes seriously the role of preaching in ministry is constantly asking himself or herself: "Just what is that blend for me and how am I doing in bringing about this interaction of biblical revelation with my personhood in a way that God's eternal Word is declared in helpful ways to all of life?"

I observe some preachers who refuse to let dogma reign over personalistic values. I observe others who see it necessary to define faith in terms of creedal fidelity. One stresses human-centeredness while the other stresses God-centeredness. One stresses natural revelation while the other stresses special revelation. One stresses a social gospel while the other stresses spiritual concerns. This has recently developed into a more subtle tension between those who are doing relational theology and those who stress cognitive theology. These themes and variations on these themes are evident in contemporary preaching.

Neither of these traditions, however, is completely consistent. There is a personalistic objectivism and a cognitive subjectivism reflected in the lifestyles, communication methods, and biblical hermeneutics of both. Nonetheless, the tension continues. At its core is an ongoing dialogue of human persons with the biblical Word that results in theological content. This dialogue ultimately produces preaching.

I view human personality as relativistic, elastic, dynamic, and subject to constant change. On the other hand, I see biblical truth as having to some extent a propositional, final, "once delivered to the saints" quality.

During the entire course of my ordained ministry I have struggled with what place my preaching should take within the context of the rest of my ministry. I am convinced that preaching is central and highly determinative of what else happens in my ministry. This leads me, then, to a continuing struggle with the place my selfhood should take in the practice of ministry, especially in preaching. I view the Bible as "the only infallible rule of faith and practice." Propositional truth is important to me, as it has been to the Church throughout its history. I believe God has chosen to reveal a great deal about himself in the Bible that can, to some extent, be captured in propositional statement.

Yet I am convinced that the cognitive restatement of those propositions, while necessary, is never exhaustive. We encounter mystery. The special personhood of God and of humans refuses to be reduced to cognitive statements. Truth, to be communicated, needs to be filtered through divine and human personality. This filtering of truth through human personality produces in me an internal creative tension. I experience the range of feelings from exhilaration to anxiety. I have given intentional focus in my preaching as well as my pastoral style to self-revelatory expression. This expression has included identification with others and personal illustrations of the truth I am endeavoring to share.

Approximately two decades into my ordained ministry, I took a study leave and worked through some of the Yale/Lyman Beecher Lectures on Preaching. I searched for insights that would authenticate or repudiate what had evolved as my own understanding of the role of preaching and the preacher in ministry, specifically as it related to my basic personal/professional self-expression. Phillips Brooks's emphasis on preaching as "communication of truth by a man to men," having the two essential elements of truth and personality, has fascinated me. I sense my need to come to a better awareness of what it means to have the truth "come really through the person, not merely over his lips, not merely into his understanding and out through his pen. It must come through his character, his affections, his whole intellectual and moral being. It must come genuinely through him."[1]

What does this really mean? How is it fleshed out in our preaching? To what extent does our use of personal experience as content and illustration in preaching enhance or detract from the communication of biblical truth? I am convinced of the truth conveyed in Brooks's concept. God has chosen to use the very person of those of us who communicate His truth to be an integral part of that truth. Who we are and how we live cannot help but detract from or enhance our preaching, and this in turn impacts every other area of our ministry. However, I believe that there is also a separateness of the Word from our personhood. We dare not identify truth so closely with our own selfhood that we relativize it in our preaching to the point that the Word of God preached is a human word cut free from the written Word. We must be careful to examine the complexities of this matter, especially in the light of our present culture's narcissistic glorification of celebrity and our own vulnerability to this temptation. We need to assess the extent and appropriateness of our homiletical endeavor to communicate truth by self to the self of others.

This is not a struggle for the preacher alone. Every person hearing the preached Word should be involved in this same struggle to find a creative intersection of biblical truth with one's own personhood. The preacher's task is to convey, with the help of the Holy Spirit, a dynamic blend of his or her person and biblical truth in a way that will facilitate a similar dialogue and ultimate intersection of the two within the hearer of the Word.

As men and women called to professional ministry, we need to be constantly measuring our effectiveness in bringing about this intersection. We should compare our own evaluative reflections of what we are trying to do with some "reality testing" as to how effective we are in doing it. As a pastor installed with responsibilities for a local congregation, I am called to serve persons who are significant participants in this divine-human interaction called preaching. I must seek to listen to the congregants, not only to judge my own effectiveness but also to take seriously what they, in their priesthood as fellow believers, have to teach me. I constantly have to ask myself how effective I am at designing, delivering, and evaluating preaching that intends to bring about an intersection between the persons—both preacher and hearer—with biblical truth. I try to keep my ear to the ground to hear honest feedback regarding my effectiveness at this task. On one occasion, I formalized this feedback enterprise in a five-stage process over a five-week period.

Stage one was the preparation of five sermons in which I entered an active dialogue with myself. In this dialogue, I dealt with the biblical text in a hermeneutical and homiletical way that proposed to mediate biblical truth through personal experience. I kept a journal describing the various ways I endeavored through each sermon to help the person in the pew wage this same struggle to blend biblical truth with personal experience.

Stage two was the preaching of the sermon. Each sermon was audiotaped and committed to writing.

Stage three was my evaluation. I reflected critically in a journal on how successful I was in accomplishing my ultimate intentions as journaled in stage one. I wrote a specific statement of what I perceived to be my strengths and weaknesses in bringing about the desired intersection of biblical truth and person in this particular preaching event.

Stage four was small-group sharing. A carefully chosen group of 12 laypersons from my church shared the ways they as hearers experienced the sermon. This group represented a variety of ages, theologies, genders, and intimacy with me. They were bound together by one common trait, their past record of willingness to speak up in honest communication. They committed themselves to meet for five, two-hour sessions in the afternoon of the Sunday each sermon was preached. The discussion was moderated by a layperson; I was not present. I did not ask this group to evaluate the sermon in any way except to critically share their experience of how the sermon, in content and delivery, enhanced or detracted from this desired intersection of biblical truth and their human persons. I communicated to them that they were not primarily evaluating me or my sermon but what transpired or did not transpire in this act of preaching to bring about this desired intersection. I listened to the cassette recordings of their discussions in an evaluation procedure, comparing what they said with my journal entries in stage one and stage three. I dealt only with the matter of the intersection of biblical truth through and to human persons and the congruence or lack of congruence of the intention with my personal evaluations and the group evaluations.

Stage five was to conclude how effective I had been in designing, delivering, and evaluating preaching that intended to effect an intersection between the preacher and hearers with biblical truth in a way that would enhance worship, pastoral care, administration, education, music, missions, and church growth.

Let me share with you the results of this ongoing process of reality testing in a way that you might find helpful for yourself. I will express it in three specific areas.

First, I am learning that my use of personal experience, illustration, and selfhood as a person in preaching does considerably enhance my communication of biblical truth. However, in certain situations, it does detract. Therefore, I must develop a continuing, positive use of my person within restraints cautioned by lay observations and my reading and research. This lesson speaks to the issue of pastoral authority.

When Phillips Brooks articulated his concept that real preaching is truth through human personality, he emphasized his conviction that truth must come through the very character affections, the whole intellectual and moral being of the preacher. This conveyance of truth through personality is not a mechanical function. He distinguished between two kinds of preachers.

> I think that, granting equal intelligence and study, there is the great difference which we feel between two preachers of the Word. The Gospel has come *over* one of them and reaches us tinged and flavored with his superficial characteristics, belittled with his littleness. The Gospel has come *through* the other, and we receive it impressed and winged with all the earnestness and strength there is in him. In the first case man has been but a printing machine or a trumpet. In the other case he has been a true man and real messenger of God.[2]

I discovered that people sense our desperate desire to apply the biblical message to ourselves and our problems prior to sharing that word with them. This builds a personal identification factor. They want to identify with the preacher who is a real person dealing with the real world in his or her own life. The hearers of the Word want to sense "believability," "credibility," and "integrity" in their preacher. Nonverbal gestures, physical bearing, eye contact, vocal variety, and the use of comic relief, all within one's normal communication style, are important to the hearer. I discovered that books of sermon illustrations are not very helpful.

Some listeners are turned off by anything that smacks of self-aggrandizing. Humility provides the counterbalance to the narcissistic tendencies of our times. Christopher Lasch puts his finger on this problem as he notes the emotional shallowness, the fear of intimacy, the false self-insight, the distorted sexuality, the dread of old age and death, which give evidence of the narcissism of many in our culture.[3] True humility demands that we preachers see ourselves as we are—sinners who have been saved by God's grace, called to renounce our era's temptation toward self-absorption, replacing it with a genuine concern for others. The preacher who is untouched by a genuine humility is extremely vulnerable to a self-delusionary narcissism.

The preacher is always incomplete. The apostle Paul talked about "knowing in part" in a way that frees us not to worry about the fact that we do not have the complete knowledge of an erudite theological professor. Humility helps us realize that our preaching is partial, our best efforts at producing the definitive sermon on a particular topic fall short. Charles Bartow emphasizes the point that a particular sermon is:

> a product of our biography, as much as it is a product of our critical theological and biblical reflection upon issues and conditions of human life. Consequently, it is a partial but not a comprehensive statement of the gospel.[4]

Humility increases our capacities to laugh at ourselves as we more clearly see our own weaknesses. We are not to be the heroes. William Willimon writes:

> The goal of sharing personal feelings, experiences, stories and anecdotes is to link people with one another, and with the text—not to link them to the preacher. It is good to ask, "Who is the hero of this story?" If the hero is the preacher, something is wrong. The hero of most biblical texts is *God,* not us. The heroes of the church are not the clergy.[5]

We have the need for integrity. Although all of us may stumble into a kind of self-deception, our urgent quest must be for integrity. I have discovered that I must be who I am. I can be no one else. I must face up to my strengths and my weaknesses. How liberating this is. This integrity conveys itself to our people, most particularly through our preaching. Then it spills over into all these other areas of our ministry. We must distinguish between the form and the message. There is a substance to be communicated that the form must not block. The stress on "total image" can develop a person who is strong on form but weak on content. We may gesture rightly, express ourselves well, have the right opinions, and appear to be consummately successful while having only memorized what looks good, not what really *is* good.

Humility and integrity are crucial safeguards to help ensure the proper use of experience, illustration, and selfhood in preaching.

Second, let me share what I am learning about biblical authority as it relates to preaching.

Although I am firmly committed to a view of biblical authority that comes under the general label "the plenary view" (a very high view of Scripture), I am discovering that I need to more carefully refine the implications of that for my preaching. I need to be increasingly aware of where my congregation is in its acceptance of biblical authority. I need to distinguish for myself between my view of Scripture as authoritative and my use of Scripture hermeneutically and homiletically, realizing that my preaching can be increasingly instructed by theological conclusions drawn by persons whose presuppositions and methodologies relating to biblical authority differ from mine.

I am discovering that people are hungry to hear what the Bible has to say as it relates to where they live today. There is great variety on any given Sunday morning in a congregation as to various views of biblical authority. The pluralism of our society has impacted the makeup of the average congregation. David H. C. Read has emphasized that there are three component parts to preaching. The first is the proclamation of the gospel. The second is the teaching of what the believer needs to know of what God has revealed. The third is ethics that tell us how to live in relationship with others. He urged that we see each sermon we preach as having all three of these elements, although the main thrust will fall into one of these three categories.

I have discovered that when I have done my exegetical research, have exposed myself to nontraditional ways of looking at the text, and have made my evaluation as to their appropriateness, I must trust the Holy Spirit to help me focus in on the key message God is trying to communicate to me and through me from that text and build the preached Word around that truth, ascertaining what is the most creative, helpful, and homiletical expression of that truth. I agree with Phillips Brooks, who wrote: "Definers and defenders of the faith are always needed, but it is bad for a church, when its ministers count it their true work to define and defend the faith rather than to preach the Gospel."[6]

Our highest calling is not that of defending the truth but proclaiming it in a proactive way with the help of the Holy Spirit, commending that eternal truth to life where it is lived today.

Third, let me share what I am learning about the Holy Spirit's capacity to use my strengths and weaknesses as a person in *process*, preaching to persons in process who are also speaking to me.

I am learning I need to trust more in the Holy Spirit's capacity to use my honest efforts and be more secure in my strengths and less afraid of my weaknesses. To state this in a slightly different way, you and I are privileged to recognize the process of sanctification in which the Holy Spirit takes our pastoral authority and, in relation to the authority of the written Word, produces a dynamic, developmental process in and through both as they intersect with the needs of a congregation.

There's a lot you and I need to know and can learn from our congregations about issues affecting preaching that we might never think to raise unless we dedicate ourselves to hearing their concerns. I am discovering I have run a little too scared throughout my ordained ministry. I am discovering that the Holy Spirit has the capacity to use my honest efforts in a way that uses my strengths and my weaknesses to positive ends. I need to listen to my critics but not let them get me down. I must reflect on my own struggle with pride and discouragement. I have a tendency to take full blame for that part of my ministry that is not well received while I tend to want to take full credit for my accomplishments. Although you and I must be willing to learn from criticism, we need to manage our tendency to allow other persons to project their pathologies on us. Most preachers have a need to please. If we do not appropriately reign in this need, we may respond to people in ways that minimize our effectiveness in ministry.

Honest acknowledgment of our human failures and our desire to uphold Jesus Christ and the Scriptures, while relating both to human need, is a tremendous safety factor. We are privileged to trust the Holy Spirit to get His message across as we exegete the text to the best of our ability and then integrate that exegesis with the existential circumstances we are preaching to.

J. Randal Nichols suggests that some ministers are over and under prepared. This, on occasion, has been my experience. I have wanted so much to do a great job of preaching that I have overresearched the commentaries, tried to pack too much into an individual sermon, and missed some of the spontaneity and delightful freshness that come from less formal study and more musing integration of the biblical message into my own experience and the experience of my congregation. Nichols wrote:

> In a word, preachers have a tendency to depend too obsessively and too long on commentaries and secondary materials and to brood and imagine too fearful and too little about what way a text or subject is trying to have with them. So you get the paradoxical and embarrassing situation of a sermon you just know had twenty hours behind it landing dead as a doornail as any kind of invitation to the Bible's world of transcendent presence, while the half-fin-

ished product of someone's insight while strap-hanging between subway stops soars like an eagle with its hearers close behind.[7]

In conclusion, the preacher and congregation must see themselves as persons whose humanness and Christian experience is lived out in community. Hell is alienation, isolation from God and each other in both this world and the next. The preacher's task is to place himself or herself and the hearers in the context of the immediate community and in the context of the broader church universal—past, present, and future. My message cannot be separated from *our* message, *my* story from *our* story. Both my story and our story are continually challenged, corrected, and transformed by *God's* story of how He works in, with, and through us. He is the God who created community—and the preacher speaks from, with, for, and to that community—as a person through whom God speaks from, with, for, and to persons. In these ways, our preaching and our roles as preachers impact every area of ministry.

Notes

1. Phillips Brooks, *Lectures on Preaching,* The Yale Lectures on Preaching, 1877 (Grand Rapids: Baker Book House, 1969), 8.

2. Ibid.

3. See Christopher Lasch, *The Culture of Narcissism* (New York: W. W. Norton and Company, 1978).

4. Charles L. Bartow, *The Preaching Moment* (Nashville: Abingdon, 1989), 62.

5. William H. Willimon, "A Funny Thing Happened to Me on the Way to the Pulpit," *The Christian Ministry* (January 1982): 7.

6. Brooks, *Lectures on Preaching,* 21.

7. J. Randall Nichols, *Building the Word* (San Francisco: Harper and Row Publishers, 1980), 31.

This chapter is adapted from of "The Role of Preaching in Ministry" in *Handbook of Contemporary Preaching,* Michael Duduit, ed. (Nashville: Broadman Press, 1992). Used by permission. All rights reserved.

Eugene H. Peterson is a writer and poet. He is professor emeritus of spiritual theology at Regent College in Vancouver, British Columbia. He has authored more than 20 books including *Leap Over a Wall, Working the Angles,* and *Under the Unpredictable Plant.* He is a contributing editor to *Leadership Journal.* Dr. Peterson is the author of the well-known *The Message,* a refreshing, contemporary version of the Bible. He was the founding pastor of Christ Our King Presbyterian Church in Bel Air, Maryland, where he ministered for 29 years.

4

Communicating the Message
"Eat This Book"
Eugene H. Peterson

CHRISTIANS FEED ON SCRIPTURE. CHRISTIANS DON'T SIMPLY LEARN or study or use Scripture; we assimilate it, take it into our lives in such a way that it gets metabolized into acts of love, cups of cold water, missions into all the world, healing and evangelism and justice in Jesus' name, hands raised in adoration of the Father.

Pastors are given responsibility for preaching these scriptures in such a way that they enter the souls of those who hear, forming lives of repentance and worship and holiness, not just lodging in the brain as information. "Eat this book," a phrase in John's Revelation, is both definitive and formative for pastors as we preach.

John is a commanding figure. He was pastor of seven little churches that were awash in the Roman world of sex and entertainment, power and violence. He didn't settle for mere survival, throwing them a plank to hold onto in the storm; he wanted them to *live*, really live—outlive everyone around them. This is what pastors do, and it is never easy. No easier now than it was for John.

In the course of the extravaganza of visions and messages that John is famous for, these wildly boisterous, rambunctious, and celebrative visions that came to him that Sunday morning as he was worshiping on the prison island of Patmos, he saw a gigantic angel, taking the cosmos for his pulpit, one foot planted in the ocean and the other on land, and holding a book in his hand from which he preached. The words in the text became thunder in the ears of John.

John was impressed, grabbed his notebook and pencil, and started to write down what he had just heard. A voice from heaven stopped him and told him to take the book and eat it. The words in the book had just been revoiced, taken off the page and set in motion in the air where they could enter ears. When John started to take what he had heard, the rolling thunder of those sentences reverberating through land and sea, take the message and write it down, why, that would be like taking the wind out of them and flattening them soundless on paper. He was stopped short. The preaching angel had just got them off the printed page, and now John is going to put them back again. No, says the heavenly voice—I want those words out there, entering ears, entering lives. I want those words preached, sung, taught, prayed—*lived*.

The voice then tells John to take the book from the angel. He takes it and the angel tells him, "Here it is. . . . Eat this book (Rev. 10:9). Get this book into your gut; get the words of this book moving through your bloodstream; chew on these words and swallow them so they can be turned into muscle and gristle and bone." And he did it; he ate the book.[1]

The book that John took and ate was the Bible.

I have a five-month-old granddaughter who eats books. When I am reading a story to her brother, she picks another off of a stack and chews on it. She is trying to get the book inside her the quickest way she knows, not through her ears but through her mouth. But soon she will go to school and be taught that that is not the way to go about it. She'll be taught to get *answers* out of her book. She'll learn to read books in order to pass examinations and having passed the exams put the book on the shelf, go out, and buy another.

But the preaching angel's book is not one that equips us to pass an examination. Eating a book assimilates it into the tissues of our lives. Readers become what they read. If Holy Scripture is to be something other than mere gossip about God, it must be internalized. John is not instructed to pass on information about God; he is commanded to assimilate the word of God so that when he speaks it will express itself artlessly in his syntax just as the food we eat, when we are healthy, is assimilated into our nerves and muscles and put to work in speech and action.

John wasn't the first biblical prophet to eat a book as if it were a peanut butter sandwich. Ezekiel was also given a book and commanded to eat it (Ezek. 2:8—3:3). Jeremiah also "ate" God's revelation, his version of the Holy Bible (Jer. 15:16). Ezekiel and Jeremiah, like John, lived in a time when there was widespread pressure to live by a text very different from the one revealed by God in these Holy Scriptures. The diet of Holy Scripture for all three of them issued in sentences of tensile strength, metaphors of blazing clarity, and a prophetic life of courageous suffering. These three rough-and-tumble prophets—John, Ezekiel, Jeremiah—responsible for the spiritual formation of God's people in the worst of times (Babylonian exile and Roman persecution) are good companions for us as we enter our pulpits week after week. Yes, *eat* this book.

The Christian community has expended an enormous amount of energy and intelligence and prayer in learning how to "eat this book" after the manner of John on Patmos, Jeremiah in Jerusalem, and Ezekiel in Babylon. We don't have to know all of it to come to the Table, but it helps to know some of it, especially since so many of our contemporaries treat it as a mere aperitif. Every word in this book is intended to do something in us, give health and wholeness, vitality and holiness, to our souls and body.

But before pastors get others to eat the book we have to eat it ourselves. We are not lecturers giving out advice or exhortation. We are preachers preparing a table of manna and quail. We are part of a holy community that for 3,000 years and more has been formed inside and out by these words of God, words that have been heard, tasted, chewed, seen, walked. Our bodies are the means of providing our souls access to God in His revelation: *Eat* this book. One of the early rabbis selected a different part of our bodies to make the same point, insisting that the primary body part for taking in the Word of God is not the ears but the feet. You learn God, he said, not through your ears but through your feet.

And so we submit our imaginations to John, sharpening our perceptions on what is involved in getting this Word of God formatively within us, wanting to do it as well as the best of our ancestors, determined not to leave any of these words in a book on a shelf, like a can of baked beans stored in a cupboard. We want to work up a good appetite, join John, and eat this book.

THE IMMENSE WORLD OF THE BIBLE

As we cultivate a participatory mind-set in relation to our Bibles, we need a complete renovation of our imaginations. We are accustomed to thinking of the biblical world as smaller than the secular world. Telltale phrases give us away. We talk of "making the Bible relevant to the world" as if the world was the fundamental reality and the Bible was something that was going to help it or fix it. We talk of "fitting the Bible into our lives" or "making room in our day for the Bible" as if the Bible were something that we can squeeze into our already full lives.

As we personally participate in the Scripture-revealed world of the emphatically personal God, we have opened our imaginations to the staggering largeness of it. Scripture expands reality far beyond anything we learned in our geography or astronomy books. Scripture breaks open our imaginations that have to take in this large, immense world of God's revelation in contrast to the small, cramped world of human "figuring out." We learn to live, imagine, believe, love, converse in this immense and richly organic and detailed world to which we are given access by our Old and New Testaments. "Biblical" does not mean cobbling texts together to prove or substantiate some dogma or practice that we have landed on. Rather it signals an opening up into "what no eye has seen, nor ear heard, nor the heart of man conceived . . . [but what] God has revealed to us through the Spirit" (1 Cor. 2:9-10, RSV).

What we must never be permitted to do, although all of us are guilty of it over and over, is force scripture to fit our experience. Our experience is too small; it's like trying to put the ocean into a thimble. What we want is to fit into the world revealed by Scripture.

What we are after is first noticing and then participating in the way the large world of the Bible absorbs the much smaller world of our science and economics and politics, the so-called "worldview" in which we are used to working out our daily concerns.[2]

We begin by abandoning all condescending approaches to the Bible. Most of us have been trained in what is sometimes termed a "hermeneutics of suspicion." People lie a lot. And people who write lie more than most. We are suspicious of everything we read, especially when it claims authority over us. And rightly so. We examine and cross-examine the text. What's going on here? What's the hidden agenda? What's behind all of this? The three modern masters of the hermeneutic of suspicion are Nietzsche, Marx, and Freud. They taught us well to take nothing at face value.

Much of this is useful. We don't want to be taken in, manipulated by clever wordsmiths, enticed to buy things we don't want and will never use by skilled publicists and advertisers, conned into some soul-destroying program by a smooth-talking propagandist. In matters that have to do with God, we are doubly on our guard, suspicious of everything and everyone, including what people write and say about the Bible. We've learned to our sorrow that religious people lie more than most others—and lies in the name of God are the worst lies of all.

But as we narrow our eyes in suspicion, the world is correspondingly narrowed down. And when we take these reading habits to our reading of Holy Scripture we end up with a small sawdust heap of facts.

Paul Ricouer has wonderful counsel for people like us. Go ahead, he says, maintain and practice your hermeneutics of suspicion. It is important to do this. Not only important, it is necessary. There are a lot of lies out there; learn to discern the truth and throw out the junk. But then reenter the book, the world, with what he calls "a second naiveté."[3] Look at the world with childlike wonder, ready to be startled into surprised delight by the profuse abundance of truth and beauty and goodness that is spilling out of the skies at every moment. Cultivate a hermeneutics of adoration—see how large, how splendid, how magnificent life is.

And then practice this hermeneutic of adoration in the reading of Holy Scripture. Plan on spending the rest of your lives exploring and enjoying the world both vast and intricate that is revealed by this text. We pray as we read, "Behold, I am the handmaid of the Lord; let it be [with] me according to your word" (Luke 1:38). Yes, *with me*.

OBEDIENCE

We enter the world of the text, the world in which God is subject, in order to become participants in the text. We have our part to play in this text, a part that is given to us by the Holy Spirit. As we play our part we become *part*-icipants.

We are given this book so that we can imaginatively and believingly enter the world of the text and follow Jesus. John Calvin in his treatment of Holy Scripture is commonly cited in this regard: "all right knowledge of God is born of obedience."[4] There is hardly a scripture exegete or translator of any standing in the Christian community who hasn't said the same thing.

If we have not entered this text as participants, we aren't going to understand what is going on. This text cannot be understood by watching from the bleachers—or even from expensive box seats. We are in on it.

I have been a runner for much of my adult life. About 15 years ago my knees gave out and I had to quit. But I miss the running; I loved the feeling of spontaneity and freedom, the relaxed rhythmic merging of my body into the world around me, the earth, the air, the wind and rain and snow that would come on long runs. And I loved the racing, the exhilaration that came in the company of other runners in 10Ks and marathons. During those years I subscribed to three different running magazines and read every book that came along by or about runners. Sometimes I would notice the oddity of what I was doing: how much is there to say about running? There aren't an infinite variety of ways you can go about it—mostly it is one foot after another. But there are aspects of training for marathons, diets, mental conditioning, caring for injuries that can also be written about. And I read everything. With a few exceptions, the writing on running is not very good, but that didn't make any difference; I was a runner, and I read it all. And then I pulled a muscle and couldn't run for a couple of months as I waited for my thigh to heal. Simultaneously, an odd thing happened. I quit reading the books and magazines. I didn't taper off, I just quit. And I didn't decide to quit, I unthinkingly quit. I didn't notice it at the time, but then I did as all these books and magazines piled up unopened, unread.

When my injury was healed and I started running my five to seven miles each day again, I resumed reading my magazines and books. Again, without thinking about it, without deciding.

And then I saw what I was doing. I was reading about running not primarily to find out something, not to learn something, but for companionship and validation and confirmation of the experience of running. Yes, I would learn a few things along the way, but mostly it was to extend and deepen and populate the world of running that I loved so much. But if I wasn't running, there was nothing to deepen.

The parallel with reading Scripture seems to me almost exact: if we are not participating in the reality revealed in the Bible, involved in the obedience Calvin wrote of, we are probably not going to be much interested in reading about it—at least not for long.

Obedience is the thing, living in active response to the living God. The most important question we ask of this text is not, "What does this mean?" but "What can I obey?" A simple act of obedience will open up our lives to this text far more quickly than any number of Bible studies and dictionaries and concordances.

Not that the study is not important. A Jewish rabbi I once studied with would often say, "For us Jews studying the Bible is more important than obeying it, because if you don't understand it rightly you will obey it wrongly and your obedience will be disobedience."

This also is true.

Gus Sikalis was a 35-year-old truck driver who became a Christian in my congregation. Gus grew up in a Greek home, conventionally Catholic, but none of it rubbed off. He left school after the eighth grade. He told me that he had never read a book. And then he became a Christian, got himself an old King James Bible with small print and read it three times in that first year of his conversion. Gus was off and running. Mary, his wife, was interested but also a bit bewildered by all this and asked a lot of questions. Mary had grown up a proper Presbyterian, gone to Sunday School all her growing up years, and was used to a religion of definitions and explanations. When Mary's questions got too difficult for Gus, he would invite me to their trailer home to help him out. One evening the subject was the parables—Mary wasn't getting it. I was trying to tell her how to read them, how to make sense out of them. I wasn't getting on very well, and Gus interrupted, "Mary, you got to live 'em, then you'll understand them—you can't figger 'em out from the outside, you got to get inside 'em; or let them git inside you."

And Gus hadn't read so much as a word of John Calvin.

THE LITURGICAL PASTOR

I want to introduce a term now that may take some time to get used to in this context: *liturgy*. As we eat this book, reading and responding, obeying and praying, as we take this all in and become participants in the text, we need the help of everyone and everything around us, for this is no private performance that we are engaged in. And we certainly are not the star of the show. *Liturgical* is the term I want to use to name the help we require. The Bible must be read liturgically.

By liturgy I don't mean what goes on in the chancel of a high Anglican church; I don't mean an order of worship; I don't mean robes and candles and incense and genuflections before the altar. Liturgy is properly used in all those settings, but I am after something else. I am after something deeper and higher and wider. I am after something that has to do with reading and preaching.

What I want is to recontextualize our reading of Scripture, our eating of this book, into a huge holy community of others. There is a millennia deep and globe-encircling community of others who are also "at table" with this book. Each time this book is assimilated formationally, the entire community—it is no exaggeration to say, the entire world—is involved and affected. The biblical story pulls the holy community into the story in a participating way.

Liturgy is the means that the church uses to stay in living touch with the living holy community as it is being formed by Holy Scripture. I want to use the word *liturgy* to refer to this intent and practice of Christians to pull everything in and out of the sanctuary into a life of worship, situate everything past and present coherently as an act of worship. Instead of limiting liturgy to the ordering of the community in discrete acts of worship, I now want to include in this comprehensive way, all the actions initiated and formed by the words in this book spread out in space and time, making connections so that our entire existence is understood liturgically, that is, connectedly, in the context of the three-personal Father, Son, and Holy Spirit.

The task of liturgy is to order the life of the holy community following the text of Holy Scripture in the world of the Trinity. It consists of two movements. First it gets us into the sanctuary, the place of adoration and attention, listening and receiving and believing before God. There is a lot involved, all the parts of our lives ordered to all aspects of the revelation of God in Jesus. Then it gets us out of the sanctuary into the world into places of obeying and loving, ordering our lives as living sacrifices in the world to the glory of God. There is a lot involved, all the parts of our lives participating in the work of salvation to the glory of God.

This is the kind of thing that John does so impressively in Revelation: presents us with everything there is, the world and our experience in it, Christ and all His angels, the devil and all his angels, heaven and hell, salvation and damnation, congregations and empires, war and peace—everything visible and invisible—and makes an act of worship out of it. He then shows how everything in that world of worship spills into the world. There are no nonparticipants. No one is standing around watching.

What John does so masterfully in Revelation, we continue from our pulpits as we stand before our holy communities.

Liturgy preserves and presents the Holy Scriptures in the context of the worshiping and obeying community of Christians who are at the center of everything God has done, is doing, and will do. The liturgy won't let us go off alone with our Bibles or self-select a few friends for Bible study and let it go at that.

The liturgical practice of the church presents us with the Holy Scriptures read and listened to and believed in the context of everything that is:

Architecture is part of it—the use of stone and timber and glass.

Color—purples and greens, reds and whites—is part of it.

Song is part of it—our hymns and anthems, our organs and orchestras.

Ancestors are part of it—the saints and scholars who enrich our preaching and prayers.

Prayer is part of it—prayers individual and corporate, voicing our deeply personal response to God, answering the call of God to praise and witness and mission.

Neighbors are part of it—these men and women and children with such different tastes and temperaments from us, many of whom we don't like very much.

And time. Liturgy gathers the holy community as it reads the Holy Scriptures into the sweeping tidal rhythms of the church year in which the story of Jesus and the Christian makes its rounds century after century, the large and easy interior rhythms of a year that moves from birth, life, death, resurrection and on to spirit, obedience, faith, and blessing. Without liturgy we lose the rhythm and get tangled in the jerky, ill-timed, and insensitive interruptions of public-relations campaigns, school openings and closings, sales days, tax deadlines, inventories, and elections. Advent is buried under "shopping days before Christmas." The joyful disciplines of Lent are exchanged for the anxious penitentials of filling out income tax forms. Liturgy keeps us in touch with the grand story as it defines and shapes our beginnings and endings, our living and dying, our rebirths and blessing in this text-formed community, visible and invisible.

When Holy Scripture is embraced liturgically, we become aware that a lot is going on all at once, a lot of people doing a lot of things. The community is on its feet, at work for God, listening and responding to the Holy Scriptures. The holy community, in the process of being formed by the Holy Scriptures is watching/listening to God's revelation taking shape before and in them as Christians follow Jesus, each person playing his or her part in the Spirit.

It is useful to reflect that the word *liturgy* did not originate in church or worship settings. In the Greek world it referred to public service, what a citizen did for the community. As the church used the word in relation to worship, it kept this "public service" quality—working for the community on behalf of or following orders from God. As we worship God, revealed personally as Father, Son, and Holy Spirit in our Holy Scriptures, we are not doing something apart from or away from the nonscripture-reading world; we do it *for* the world, bringing all creation and all humanity before God, presenting our bodies and all the beauties and needs of humankind before God in praise and intercession, penetrating and serving the world for whom Christ died in the strong name of the Trinity.

Liturgy puts us to work along with all the others who have been and are being put to work in the world by and with Jesus, following our spirituality-forming text. Liturgy keeps us in touch with all the action that has been and is being generated by the text. Liturgy prevents the narrative form of Scripture from being reduced to private individualized consumption.

Understood this way "liturgical" has little to do with choreography in the chancel or an aesthetics of the sublime. It is obedient, participatory listening to Holy Scripture in the company of the holy community through time (our 2,000 years of responding to this text) and in space (our friends in Christ all over the world). High church Anglicans, revivalistic Baptists, hands-in-the-air praising Charismatics, and Quakers sitting in a bare room in silence are all required to read and live this text liturgically, participating in the holy community's reading of Holy Scripture. There is nothing "churchy" or elitist about it; it is a vast and dramatic "storying," taking our place in the story and letting everyone else have their part in the story also, making sure that we don't leave anything or anyone out of the story. Without sufficient liturgical support and structure we are very apt to edit the story down to fit our individual tastes and predispositions.

VIRTUOSO LIVING

Frances Young uses the extended analogy of music and its performance to provide a way of understanding the interrelated complexities of reading and living the Holy Scriptures, what I am calling "eating the book." Her book *Virtuoso Theology* searches out what she names as "the complex challenges involved in seeking authenticity in performance."[5] It is of the very nature of music that it is to be "performed." Performance, though, does not consist in accurately reproducing the notes in the score as written by the composer, although it includes this. Everyone recognizes the difference between an accurate but wooden performance of, say, Mozart's Violin Concerto No. 1, and a virtuoso performance by Itzhak Perlman. Perlman's performance is not distinguished merely by his technical skill in reproducing what Mozart composed; he wondrously enters into and conveys the spirit and energy—the "life"— of the score. Significantly, he adds nothing to the score, neither "jot nor tittle." Even though he might reasonably claim that with access to the interrelated psychologies of music and sexuality he understands Mozart much better than Mozart understood himself, he restrains himself; he does not interpolate.

One of the continuous surprises of musical and dramatic performance is the sense of fresh spontaneity that comes in the performance: faithful attention to the text does not result in slavish effacement of personality; rather it releases what is inherent in the text itself as the artist performs; "music has to be 'realized' through performance and interpretation."[6]

Likewise Holy Scripture. The two analogies, performing the music and eating the book, work admirably together. The complexity of the performance analogy supplements the earthiness of the eating analogy (and vice versa) in directing the pastor to lead the holy community into the world of Holy Scripture formationally.

But if we are "unscripted," Alisdair McIntyre's word in this context,[7] we spend our lives as anxious stutterers in both our words and actions. When, though, we do this rightly—performing the score, eating the book—embracing the holy community that internalizes this text, we are released into freedom: "I will run in the way of thy commandments when thou enlargest my understanding" (Ps. 119:32, RSV).

Notes

1. For further discussion of "assimilation" reading, see Eugene H. Peterson, _Working the Angles_ (Grand Rapids: William B. Eerdmans, 1987), 87-148.

2. See Karl Barth, "The Srange New World Within the Bible" in _The Word of God and the Word of Man_ (Gloucester: Peter Smith, 1924), 28-50.

3. Paul Ricoeur, _The Symbolism of Evil_ (Boston: Beacon Press, 1969), 351-52.

4. John Calvin, _Institutes of the Christian Religion_, tran. F. L. Battles (Philadelphia: Westminster Press, 1960), I.6.2.

5. Frances Young, _Virtuoso Theology_ (Cleveland: Pilgrim Press, 1993), 21.

6. Ibid., 22. The "performance analogy has also been used effectively by Nicholas Lash, "Performing the Scriptures" in _Theology on the Way to Emmaus_ (SCM Press, 1986) and Brian Jenner, "Music to the Sinner's Ear?" _Epworth Review_, xvi (1989), 35-38.

7. Alisdair McIntyre, _After Virtue_ (Notre Dame, Ind.: U of Notre Dame Press, 1981), 216.

For Further Reading

Barth, Karl. _The Word of God and the Word of Man_. Tran. Douglas Horton. Gloucester, Mass.: Peter Smith, 1978 [original German publication, 1924].

Ellul, Jacques. _The Humiliation of the Word_. Grand Rapids: William B. Eerdmans, 1985.

Farrer, Austin. _The Glass of Vision_. Westminster: Dacre Press, 1948.

Fee, Gordon. _Listening to the Spirit in the Text_. Grand Rapids: William B. Eerdmans, 2000.

Frye, Northrop. _The Great Code_. New York: Harcourt Brace Jovanovich, 1982.

Illich, Ivan. _In the Vineyard of the Text_. Chicago: University of Chicago Press, 1993.

Young, Francis. _Virtuoso Theology_. Cleveland: Pilgrim Press, 1993.

Haddon W. Robinson, Ph.D., is the Harold John Ockenga Distinguished Professor of Preaching at Gordon-Conwell Theological Seminary. The author of the immensely popular textbook, *Biblical Preaching* (now in second edition), he has influenced thousands of evangelical preachers through his writing and through his former students who now teach homiletics. A native of New York City, Dr. Robinson completed graduate studies at Dallas Theological Seminary (Th.M.), Southern Methodist University (M.A.,) and the University of Illinois (Ph.D.).

A former professor of homiletics at Dallas Theological Seminary and former president of Denver Seminary, in 1991 he assumed the distinguished faculty assignment at Gordon-Conwell Theological Seminary, his current assignment at the time of this publication. He also directs the Doctor of Ministry Program at Gordon-Conwell. Dr. Robinson was named 1 of the 12 most effective preachers in the English-speaking world in a 1996 Baylor University poll. He is one of the hosts for *Discover the Word* (formerly *Radio Bible Class*), a daily radio program broadcast 600 times a day on stations around the world. He is a senior consulting editor of *Preaching* magazine and a fellow and senior editor for *Christianity Today.* His book *Biblical Preaching* is currently being used as a text for preaching in over 120 seminaries and Bible colleges throughout the world.

5

What Is Expository Preaching?

Haddon W. Robinson

❧ THE CHURCH IN THE 21ST CENTURY DESPERATELY NEEDS BIBLICAL preaching. However, not everyone agrees with the verdict. The word is out in some circles that preaching should be abandoned. The moving finger has passed it by, we are told, and it is now pointing to other methods and other ministries that are more "effective" and up to date.

To explain why preaching has been discredited would take us into every area of our common life. For one thing, the image of the preacher has changed. No longer is he or she regarded as the intellectual and spiritual leader in the community. Ask the man in the pew what a preacher is, and his description may not be flattering. Kyle Haselden is afraid that some people have an image of the preacher at "a bland composite which shows the pastor as the congregation's congenial, ever helpful, ever ready to help boy scout; as the darling of old ladies and as sufficiently reserved with the young ones; as the father image for young people and a companion to lonely men, as the affable glad hander at teas and civic club luncheons."[1]

In addition, preaching has lost support because it takes place in an overcommunicated society that bombards us with a hundred thousand "messages" a day. Television and radio feature pitchmen delivering "a word from the sponsor" with all the sincerity of the evangelist. In that context a preacher may sound like another salesman who, in Ruskin's words, "plays stage tricks with the doctrines of life and death."

Add to these reasons the reality that liberalism has robbed the person in the pulpit of an authoritative message. Fads in communication have become more important than truth. Multimedia presentations, films, videos, sharing sessions, colored lights, and modern music may be symptoms of either health or disease. Certainly, modern methods can enhance communication, but often they are used because there is no message at all—and the unusual somehow masks the vacuum.

Then, too, action appeals to us more than talk and listening. "Stop preaching at me" we say, and that reveals our irritation with preaching. Preaching in some churches is regarded as little more than a "necessary evil" that goes with being a Christian. People with this attitude may conclude the apostles had things backward when they observed, "It is not right that we should forsake the Word of God to serve tables." In our day of activism, there is a temptation to declare, "It is not right that we should forsake the service of tables to preach the Word of God."

TAKING SCRIPTURE SERIOUSLY

No one who takes the Scriptures seriously, however, dares to count preaching out. Paul was a writer. From his pen we have the inspired letters of the New Testament. Heading the list of his writings is his Epistle to the Romans. Measured by its impact upon history, few documents can compare with it. But when Paul wrote this letter to the congregation in Rome, he confessed, "I long to see you, that I may impart to you some spiritual gift to strengthen you, that is, that we may be mutually encouraged by each other's faith, both yours and mine" (1:11-12, RSV). Some ministries cannot take place apart from face-to-face contact. Even the writing of an inspired letter is not a substitute. "I am eager to preach the gospel to you also who are in Rome" (1:15, RSV). Power exists in the word spoken that the written word cannot replace.

Preaching in the minds of the New Testament writers is God in action. Peter, for example, reminded his readers that they had "been born anew, not of perishable seed but of imperishable, through the living and abiding word of God" (1 Pet. 1:23, RSV). How did this word come to do its work in their lives? "That word," Peter explains, was "the good news which was preached to you." Through preaching they were redeemed.

Paul wrote of the Thessalonians that "they turned to God from idols, to serve a living and true God, and to wait for his Son from heaven" (1 Thess. 1:9-10, RSV). This "about face" occurred, says the apostle, because "when you received the Word of God which you heard from us, you accepted it not as the word of men but as what it actually is, the word of God, which is at work in you believers" (1 Thess. 2:13, RSV). Preaching, therefore, was not merely talk about God. It was God himself working through the message and personality of the preacher confronting men and women and bringing them to himself.

This explains why in 2 Tim. 4:2 Paul encourages his young associate Timothy to "preach the word." The word for "preach" means "to cry out, herald, or exhort." It is as though the message should so stir a person that it must be poured out with passion and fervor. Not all passion-ate pleading from the pulpit, however, has divine authority. While a preacher must be a "herald"—he or she must herald the Word. Any-thing less cannot legitimately be called preaching.

The constant temptation of the preacher is to cry out some other message than the Scriptures—a political system, a theory of economics, a new religious philosophy. No matter that this may be done in authori-tative tones, a preacher who does not preach the Scriptures abandons his or her authority and no longer confronts people with the Word of God but simply speaks another human word.

God speaks through the Scriptures to all people in all times. The Bible is not merely "the old, old story" of what God did in some other time and place, nor is it only a statement of ideas about God—inspired and inerrant. The Bible is God's tool of communication through which He addresses men and women today. Through the Scriptures, God brings us to salvation (2 Tim. 3:15) and to a richness and ripeness of Christian character (vv. 16-17).

DEFINING EXPOSITORY PREACHING

The type of preaching that most effectively lays open the Bible so that people are confronted by its truth is expository preaching. At its best, expository preaching is "the communication of a biblical concept, derived from and transmitted through a historical, grammatical, and lit-erary study of a passage in its context, which the Holy Spirit applies first to the personality and experience of the preacher, then through him or her to the listeners."

This definition has several parts. First of all, the substance of the ex-pository sermon is derived from the Scriptures. The expositor realizes that although the Bible is a book like no other book, it is still a book. In fact, it is a collection of writings that can be studied like other literature. R. A. Montgomery, in his book *Expository Preaching,* makes this point:

> The preacher undertakes the presentation of particular books [of the Bible] as some men would undertake the latest best seller. The preacher seeks to bring the message of definite units of God's word to his people. He discovers the main theme or constituent parts of the book's message as they were in the mind of the writer. . . . His treatment of words, phrases, texts, portions is important not only for what they may say separately, but as they relate to the main theme of the writer and the end he had in view in writing this book.[2]

In a larger sense, therefore, expository preaching is more a philosophy than a method. It is the answer to a basic question: "Does the preacher subject his or her thought to the Scriptures, or does he or she subject the Scriptures to his or her thought?" Is the passage used like the national anthem at a football game—it gets things started but then is not heard again? Or is the text the essence of the sermon to be exposed to the people?

Though it is possible to preach an orthodox sermon without explaining a biblical passage, unfolding a portion of Scripture guards the preacher's thought against heresy. Doing this regularly, it forces the preacher to speak to the many issues of life dealt with in the Scriptures that he or she otherwise might easily overlook. Above all, the preacher speaks with an authority not his or her own, and the person in the pew will have a better chance to hear God speak to him or her directly.

A second important factor in the definition involves the means by which the biblical message is communicated to the congregation. The preacher transmits it on the same basis by which he or she received it. In the study, the expositor examines the grammar, history, and context of the passage. In the pulpit, the preacher must deal with enough of the language, background, and setting of the text so that an attentive listener is able to check the message from the Bible.

As a result, effective expository preaching will be occupied largely with the explanation of Scripture. A good expository sermon will reflect the passage not only in its central message but also in its development, purpose, and mood. As this takes place, people not only learn the Bible as they listen but are also stimulated to study the Scriptures for themselves.

SCRIPTURES OF EXPOSITORY PREACHING

Expository preaching offers great benefits to the preacher. For one thing, it gives the preacher truth to preach. Many ministers spend a frustrating part of their week "starting to get underway to begin" their sermon preparation. Only a genius can think up enough original material that is fresh and stimulating and that will keep the same audience interested 100 times a year. The person who draws topics from his or her own mind and experience dabbles in a puddle. The man or woman who expounds the Scripture does business in great waters.

Expository preaching provides the preacher with many types of sermons. A single verse may be expounded (Alexander McLaren was outstanding in this respect). A passage may be expounded—this is what is usually considered as expository preaching. In addition, he or she may trace a topic or doctrine through the Bible. To do this, the preacher finds the many places in which a topic or doctrine is considered. First, the topic is related to the particular passage in which it is found, then it is related to the other passages. Biographical preaching may also be expository. Much of the Scripture comes to us in the form of history or biography. If six men are taken out of Genesis, for example, there is not much left.

Our definition tells us that expository preaching also develops the preacher into a mature Christian. When an expositor studies the Bible, the Holy Spirit probes the preacher's life. As a preacher prepares sermons, God prepares the person. Alexander McLaren said that everything he was, he owed to the fact that day after day he studied the Scriptures. As the expositor masters a passage, he or she will discover the truth of that passage in the hand of the Spirit who masters him or her. P. T. Forsyth understood this when he wrote: "The Bible is the supreme preacher to the preacher."[3]

THE PURPOSE OF EXPOSITORY PREACHING

Finally, the basic purpose of expository preaching is the basic purpose of the Bible. It takes place so that through it the Holy Spirit may change people's lives and destinies. Preaching and teaching, of course, are not the only means by which God builds His people, but they are His major means. The effective expositor knows that God is not speaking to people today about the Bible as though it were a textbook in history or archaeology. The Holy Spirit speaks to men and women today about themselves from the Bible. The person in the pulpit or those in the pew do not sit in judgment on Judas or David or Peter or Solomon. Under the teaching of Scripture, they must judge themselves.

To carry out this purpose, the expositor must know not only the message but also the people to which it will be delivered. He or she must exegete both the Scriptures and the congregation. Imagine that Paul's letters to the Corinthians had gotten lost in the mail and had reached the Christians in Philippi instead. Those people would have been perplexed at what Paul wrote. The believers in Philippi lived in situations different from their brethren at Corinth. The letters of the New Testament, like the prophecies of the Old Testament, were addressed to specific people living in particular situations.

"Doctrines must be preached practically, and duties doctrinally," was the way our Protestant forebears put it. Perhaps this is the largest problem in what is called expository preaching today. The preacher lectures about the "there and then" as though God lived back in the "once upon a time" and fails to bring the eternal truth to focus on the attitudes and actions of people in the "here and now." Application is not incidental to effective expository preaching, it is crucial!

In relating the Bible to experience, however, the expositor dares not twist the Scriptures to fit people's lives. Instead he or she calls men and women to bring themselves into subjection to the standards of the Bible. Christians must conform to the age to come, not to this present age. The application moves both ways. Biblical truth must be related to people's lives, but on the other hand, people's lives must be changed to be relevant to biblical faith.

CONCLUSION

F. B. Meyer, himself a gifted expositor, understood the awe with which a biblical preacher approaches his task: "He is in line of great succession. The Reformers, the Puritans, the pastors of the Pilgrim fathers were essentially expositors. They did not announce their own particular opinions, which might be a matter of private interpretation or doubtful disposition; but, taking their stand on Scripture, drove home their message with irresistible effect with, 'Thus said the Lord!'"[4]

The major problems of our society are ultimately spiritual. Men and women always stand in desperate need of God. "They will not ask for help, unless they believe in Him, and they will not believe in Him unless they have heard of Him, and they will not hear of Him unless they get a preacher, and they will never have a preacher unless one is sent. But as the Scripture says the footsteps of those who bring good news is a welcome sound. . . . So faith comes from what is preached, and what is preached comes from the Word of Christ" (Rom. 10:14-17, NJB).

Notes

1. Kyle Haselden, *The Urgency of Preaching* (New York: Harper and Row, 1963), 89.

2. R. A. Montgomery, *Expository Preaching* (New York: Revell, 1939), 42.

3. P. T. Forsyth, *Positive Preaching and the Modern Mind* (London and New York: Independent, 1907), 11.

4. F. B. Meyer, *Expository Preaching Plans and Methods* (1910; Grand Rapids: Zondervan, 1954), 58.

For Further Reading

Forsyth, P. T. *Positive Preaching and the Modern Mind.* London and New York: Independent, 1907.

Haselden, Kyle. *The Urgency of Preaching.* New York: Harper and Row, 1963.

Meyer, F. B. *Expository Preaching Plans and Methods.* 1910; Grand Rapids: Zondervan, 1954.

Montgomery, R. A. *Expository Preaching.* New York: Fleming H. Revell, 1939.

Stott, John R. W. *Between Two Worlds: The Art of Preaching in the Twentieth Century.* Grand Rapids: Eerdmans, 1982.

This chapter is reprinted from *Bibliotheca Sacra* 131:521 (January—March 1974) : 55-60. Reprinted by permission. "What Is Expository Preaching?" was also published in Haddon W. Robinson, *Making a Difference in Preaching,* Scott M. Gibson, ed. (Grand Rapids: Baker Books, 1999), 61-68.

Elizabeth R. Achtemeier, Ph.D., was a nationally-known scholar and preacher. She passed away October 25, 2002, several months following her signing a writing agreement for this chapter.

Dr. Achtemeier was a Phi Beta Kappa graduate of Stanford University and received her theological education at Union Theological Seminary in New York. She did post-graduate work at Heidelberg University in Germany and Basel University in Switzerland before earning the Doctor of Philosophy degree in Old Testament from Columbia University in 1959.

Dr. Achtemeier served as adjunct professor of Bible and homiletics at Union Theological Seminary in Virginia from 1973 to 1996 where her husband, Paul J. Achtemeier, also served on the faculty as professor of New Testament. Elizabeth Achtemeier also served as a visiting professor at Gettysburg Lutheran Seminary, Pittsburgh Theological Seminary, and Duke Divinity School. From 1959-73 she taught Old Testament theology at Lancaster Theological Seminary in Pennsylvania.

She was the author of 20 books, including *The Old Testament Roots of Our Faith,* with Paul J. Achtemeier. Other titles include *Nature, God, and Pulpit; Preaching from the Old Testament; The Committed Marriage;* and *Preaching About Family Relationships.* She was a frequent contributor to biblical dictionaries, scholarly journals, and various church publications.

Known throughout the United States and Canada as an outstanding preacher, lecturer, and scholar, she was frequently invited to speak to congregations, church conferences and various universities, including Harvard, Princeton, Duke, Yale, Smith, and Wellesley.

6

Preaching the Authority of the Canon

Elizabeth R. Achtemeier

🌿 BY THE GRACE OF GOD, WHO DIRECTS OUR LIVES ACCORDING TO A kindly providence, I had the privilege of teaching homiletics to men and women for 40 years in several seminaries. I always considered the vocation of preaching the high-water mark of seminary education, because it called on all of the learning that students had acquired in other classes—their knowledge of the Bible, their theological training, their understanding of church history, their educational and pastoral skills. All of those disciplines had to work together in the students' sermons. I always considered myself more fortunate than other seminary professors, because when the students preached in class, I could clearly see their actual growth as homileticians, a growth not evident in other classes. I'll never forget the one young man whose mouth was so dry from fright when he preached for the first time that he had to stop in the middle of a sentence and go out and get a drink of water. But today he is an outstanding preacher. Others actually trembled in the pulpit, though some mounted the pulpit as if they owned the world. The experience of teaching these men and women, however, was a blessed one. I learned a great deal.

One of my greatest joys in retirement years has been to speak in churches being led by some of those former students and watch them minister to their people with faith and energy, with dedication and love, and with strength in the Holy Spirit. There are some very fine sermons being preached from some pulpits, both large and small, in this country. In that I find joy. That is true of some sermons and pulpits, but certainly not all.

There are still preachers across the land who cannot think in a straight line—cannot move logically from one point in the sermon to the next. So they wander from subject to subject, and the congregation has no idea where they are going. Other ministers love to tell stories—very long stories—that bring their sermons to a complete halt and lead the listeners to conclusions entirely different from what is intended in the biblical text. Some preachers give performances in the pulpit. They concentrate so much on themselves that not a glimpse of the Lord can be seen behind their grand persona. Still other preachers despise their congregations and love to dump judgment on them. There are those who commit one of the greatest sins of the pulpit—they bore their people. Some preachers never preach from the Old Testament or from the Epistles of the New. There are the moralizers, allegorists, psychologists, sociologists, even humanists and atheists—all wasting the glorious opportunity to preach the gospel to the largest captive audience in the world. Numerous congregations are left hungry for the bread of life, wandering aimlessly through meaningless lives, bearing life's suffering without a Shepherd to comfort, to rescue, to redeem. The apostle Paul wrote, "Faith comes from what is heard, and what is heard comes by the preaching of Christ. . . . . And how are they to hear without a preacher?" (Rom. 10:17, 14, RSV).

So what should we say about preaching? The Triune God makes himself known to us through the witness of the Scripture, through the confession of faith made up of 66 books that the Church has called our canon. One of the most important aspects of that canon is that it comes to us as a historical narrative. None of it, of course, is "pure history," if there is such a thing. The Scriptures are interpreted history, not coldly factual accounts. But all of the writings of the canon, including the psalms, the prophets, the wisdom writings, and epistles and apocalypses —all have their context in the ongoing story that has its beginning in God and that moves toward God's completion of it.

The historical nature of the Bible mirrors the nature of God. In our time, we all are prone to turn God into an object to be discussed. For example, in the story of Eve's conversation with the serpent in Gen. 3, we turn God into an immovable someone "out there." We discuss Him. We theologize about Him. We defend Him. Sometimes we question Him. We call our people to trust Him. He's there, an object to be talked about. But that is not the case in the Scriptures. God is an active God, always on the move, always pressing forward toward His goal of a new community on a new earth, called the kingdom of God. All of those verbs that describe His action become the most important words in the Bible.

So we have in the Scriptures clearly delineated focal points where God breaks into human history and moves His purpose forward. Those points are easily outlines. In the Old Testament, God creates a world that is very good, but when it is corrupted by human sin, the Lord sets out through His people Israel to make it very good again. We read of Israel's slavery, the Exodus, the wilderness wandering, the gift of the Promised Land, the Davidic kingship, the prophets, the exiles, and the promises of future salvation in a new age, with the psalmists, wisdom writers, and seers recording their responses to it all.

With the birth of Jesus in Bethlehem, the whole word of God to Israel is gathered up and incarnated, and the announcement is made that the new age of the kingdom of God, promised in the Old Testament, has broken into human history in the person of our Lord. In Jesus' ministry in Galilee and Judea, the powers of God's new age work their teaching and healing and reaching. At His death, the sin and corruption of the old age struggle for supremacy and lose. And on Easter morn, death itself and the power of sin are broken and vanquished by God in Christ, the sole Victor. The Spirit of God in Christ to the disciples at Pentecost after the Lord's ascension sends the good news of God's new age of victory forth to Judea and Samaria and the ends of the earth. The risen Christ transforms a man named Saul. He becomes Paul the apostle and goes forth to establish and guide churches in Galatia, Asia Minor, and Macedonia. Letters are sent by sea and on Roman roads. Oral traditions are gathered into Gospels. Little churches, following the traditions of Paul or John, of Hebrews or James or Matthew, gather as points of light in the midst of the darkness of a pagan world. Persecution by the state and by the Jews does not silence their gospel. John of Patmos looks forward to the full coming of the Kingdom, where there is a new heaven and a new earth, and all the kingdoms of this world have become the kingdom of our Lord and of His Christ.

This is all a history, an ongoing story of God's working through 2,000 years of history, and every text in the Scriptures has as its context that ongoing story. It seems perverse, then, for any preacher to turn the story into a set of propositions, to which assent is sought if the listener wants to be called a Christian. Propositional preaching paralyzes an action or characteristic of God, transforms it into a dogma, and makes it an object to be believed on the preacher's advice. Woe to the poor parishioner who will not accept the advice! What has really happened is that the preacher has usurped the action of God toward the congregation and has replaced it with a dead truth to be accepted. Or the preacher transforms the story into a psychological or sociological "truth" to be used in the analysis of society's ways.

The narrative that comes to us through the Scriptures is neither dead dogma nor psychological or sociological truths, however. It is action-bearing Word of God. When God speaks His word and works His works through the Bible's confession, He does not just convey new information or tell of an interesting event. He continues to work in the life of the gathered congregation. The Word of God that comes to us through the Bible is active, effective force, which brings about a new situation. For example, in Gen. 1, God says, "Let there be light," and light is created. Or in Isa. 55, the Word of God does not return to Him void, but accomplishes that which God purposes. The Word works, bringing about that of which it speaks. The amazing thing about the Bible is that the action of God's Word is not limited to the biblical world in the past. The great Lutheran preacher Paul Scherer once remarked, "God didn't stop acting when his book went to press." The Word of God, spoken through the Scriptures, continues to act in the lives of all who will hear it, transforming them and bringing about in their persons and their society a new situation. The word of the past becomes contemporary in our present, continuing to work out God's purpose of salvation in our lives and world, until finally the kingdom of God will be realized fully in God's plan for history and nature.

This is to say that preaching, if it is biblical preaching—preaching the Word of God from the Scriptures—is sacramental. Through the preached Word, God acts toward His gathered congregation. In worship we bring our *sacrifices*—sacrifices of praise and thanksgiving. In worship we also experience *sacraments*. These are the life-giving actions that God extends to us. Preaching has as its purpose the mediation or conveyance of God's action toward us. Preaching is sacramental. Through it, God works in our lives.

Unfortunately, all too much preaching leaves people as they are. In the worst cases, the pulpit simply entertains a congregation or gives them an emotional "high." Some—though not all—of the popular contemporary praise services serve that purpose. The instrumental music with its beat, the clapping, the sentimental prayers, the exuberant expressions of praise draw the people into crowd excitement that raises spirits but changes personalities not at all. In some churches therapeutic preaching serves to assure the congregation that they are loved and accepted as they are and are really fine people who perhaps need just a little psychological adjustment to be happy. Moralizing preaching simply conveys little stories with moral points about how to get along in life, much like a *Reader's Digest* article or an Aesop fable. In much of this pulpiteering a congregation remains unchanged, and the active Word of God from the biblical text is not allowed to work.

But if the Word of God is an active, effective force, bringing about a new situation—if it is truly, as Jeremiah says (23:29), like a hammer that breaks rocks in pieces or like a fire burning in one's bones—then the purpose of a sermon is so to convey that work that it is given freedom to act and to change its hearers. The sermon becomes the medium of God's action on His people, and they are left, not as they wish, but as God wills.

God's action among His people through the medium of the sermon may take any one of a number of forms. The Lord may simply deepen the faith of some saint in the congregation—and every congregation has such a person or persons. God may increase our love for one another so that we are bound more truly into a community, or He may send us forth into greater service to our society. The Lord may call our lifestyle into serious question and bring the terrifying weight of His judgment upon us. He may comfort us in some distress. He may erase some guilt or forgive some sin or flood our hearts with His Spirit. The Lord may even overwhelm a parishioner with an awesome sense of His glory and majesty, so that there is the momentary feeling of standing with one foot in heaven. Or God may tenderly assure us that underneath always are His everlasting arms. The work of God through His Word calls forth all our responses in His worship—our repentance, our confession of faith, our praise and petitions and thanksgiving, and above all, our surrender and our commitment of our lives to Him alone. Whatever God chooses to do with His people through the words of His preacher, those people do not remain the same persons they were when they entered the church. God's Word, faithfully preached, transforms human lives and congregations when God so wills by His Spirit. God uses that transformation in His ongoing plan of salvation.

Perhaps the most sweeping transformation that is wrought by God's Spirit in a congregation through the preaching of the active, biblical Word, however, is in the congregation's total worldview. There is a lot of talk these days about spirituality—and that word is given all sorts of meanings. It seems to me that true spirituality consists in having one's total worldview transformed.

Our people live in an almost totally secular society. That is, they and we live in a society from which it is thought God is absent. That view is fostered, of course, by the almost total elimination of the mention of the Christian God in public life—in our schools, in our media, in our law courts, in our ethics, in our universities, in our public assemblies—because of the influence of the ACLU and others. As a result, our people no longer believe with the prophets of the Old Testament that the Lord God is in charge of international relations. No. The politicians, the military, the multinational corporations all control what happens to nations, they think, and so the whole populace is left with the thought that some terrorist may blow us all to kingdom come.

In the same manner, most people no longer believe with the whole biblical testimony that God is Lord over nature. While our scientists have not quite figured out what happened at the "big bang," many persons are quite certain that the natural world runs automatically. They are all deists. Natural laws direct the course of nature's evolution and yearly cycle. The only ones who can solve all of nature's mysteries, they believe, are the scientists—though faith in their ability to save us has weakened. But God does not interfere in nature's laws. In many persons' view, miracles and resurrection are fables. To hear from the Scriptures that God not only created the world but also sustains all its processes, using them in His purpose, is therefore quite absurd to the thinking of many 21st-century souls, just as is the biblical view that nature, too, is in need of redemption.

As for our personal lives, the American populace is noted for its piety and its belief that there is some sort of divine being who watches over us and who can help us out of our jams. These days that divine being is imagined in all sorts of ways. When it comes to our individual lives, however, the biblical thought of the divine fellowship of the Trinity bumps up against our widespread individualism. Everyone goes it alone and there is little understanding that God's goal in the Bible is to make a new community that lives in faithfulness and righteousness under God's guiding Lordship. We take our directions from the psychological and medical experts, the marriage counselors, the child guidance authorities, Martha Stewart, the latest fads around us, the media, and maybe even Dear Abby.

But a biblical faith, inspired by the Word of God, changes all of that, and we come to see that we live in a God-haunted world, where no event is beyond God's Lordship, where no word or action escapes His view, where we are beset behind and before by the Lord, and not a word is on our tongue but God knows it altogether. If we ascend to heaven, He is there. If we make our bed in hell, God is there. He reigns over His creation as its Lord, its King, its Master, its Redeemer, its God of all life, who loves His world so much that He gives His only begotten Son, that whoever believes in Him will never perish, but have life eternal in His good company. I think biblical preaching can bring about such a worldview. It can, by the work of the Spirit of Christ, transform our understanding of everything. For if anyone is in Christ, that person is a new creation, and the community in which they worship is the covenant people of the Lord our God.

So finally, everything depends on engaging the biblical text—on so entering into the scripture for the day that its text becomes the Word of God, spoken immediately to preacher and to the congregation.

Perhaps one of the frequent mistakes that you and I make in our preaching is to talk _about_ a text. Some don't bother with a text at all! Many of us, however, stand back from our scripture and discuss it as an object. "Our text says," we say repeatedly in the sermon. Or "the person in this text thought so-and-so." Or "the psalmist experienced such-and-such." We stand off from the text and observe it. But so much of the Bible is direct address. So much of it is the Word of God spoken directly to us, God using His scriptures to speak to our hearts and minds and to our situations. That is true even of many passages in the Old Testament. For example, when God says to northern Israel in the time of Amos, "You only have I known of all the families of the earth; therefore I will punish you for all your iniquities" (Amos 3:2, RSV), that is not just the Lord's announcement to Israel in the 8th century B.C. That's also His word spoken to us, in our congregations, in the 21st century. After all, according to the apostle Paul, we are the new Israel in Jesus Christ (Gal. 6:16). Thus, God's words and actions toward His covenant people Israel are also frequently words and actions toward us. The task of the preacher using Amos, then, is to mediate that prophet's words as the contemporary Word and action of God toward His gathered people in the church on Sunday morning.

Everything depends on getting inside the text, on so absorbing its meaning, its emphases, its structure, its message, that it becomes, by the grace of the Spirit, the living, immediate Word of the living, present God for the assembled people of God. How do we do that?

Obviously, I cannot fully answer that question. It takes a lot of prayer, a lot of meditation, a lot of trust in the action of the Word of God, and the gracious working of the Holy Spirit. I can, though, give you at least a partial accounting of a method that I have found to be very helpful and that has forced me to stick to the scriptural text and not go wandering off to the far country of my own thoughts.

The method is called the rhetorical analysis—the study of the rhetorical structure of a biblical text. This method looks at the words of the text, preferably in the Hebrew or Greek, but you can also do it with the English translation. You note the repetition of words, exclamations, questions, parallelisms, inclusions, imperatives, adversatives, contrasts, the use of particles and participles, strophic structure in poetry—all of the features of the language used in the text. All of these features illumine the emphases of the passage and enable you to get into its thought.

Consider some examples. Look at Deut. 8:7-20. This is the Old Testament text for Thanksgiving Day in Cycle A of the three-year lectionary. Some preachers use this text to make the congregation feel guilty about all of the luxuries we enjoy in the United States. Look, though, at the repetitions in the text. Repetitions are always important, because the Bible repeats words and phrases for emphasis. So, we have:

"The LORD your God" in verses 7, 10, 11, 14, 18, 19, 20.

"[Lest you] forget" in verses 11, 14, 19. "Remember" is its corollary in verse 18. The major thrust of the text is to remember and not forget. What else is thanksgiving but remembering—remembering and not forgetting all of the things the Lord our God has done? Indeed, throughout the Old Testament, it is said that Israel loses her faith when she forgets God's actions.

In this text for Thanksgiving Day, the basis of thanksgiving is remembering all the good deeds that the Lord has done. Thanksgiving has its foundation in remembering. We, of course, have lots of gracious deeds of the Lord to remember. That can form the content of your sermon.

As another example, look at the use of little particles in the hymns of the Bible—*ki* in the Hebrew, *oti* in the Greek—often translated with the little word "for," meaning "because," or sometimes translated "that." The important function of that little word is to give the reason for the statement that precedes it. Look at Ps. 98: "O sing to the LORD a new song, / for he has done marvelous things! / His right hand and his holy arm / have gotten him victory" (v. 1, RSV). The phrase beginning with "for" tells the reason for praising God. So can you think of a victory that the Lord has won as a reason for your people to praise Him? A student gave a seminary chapel talk in which he did nothing but admonish us to praise God. I called him in afterward and told him that he had urged us to praise but given us no reason to do so. The "for" phrase in this psalm gives us a reason, and that points you to your sermon.

Look at verses 8-9 of this same psalm: "Let the floods clap their hands; / let the hills sing together for joy together / before the LORD, for he comes to judge the earth. / He will judge the world with righteousness, / and the peoples with equity" (RSV). All of nature here is called to praise, because God—Christ in His second coming—is coming with His final judgment. And the nature of that judgment will be righteous and equitable. Is that not a reason for the creation's praise in an evil world such as ours? The content of your sermon is pointed out to you by the psalm's structure, a structure that is also found, for example, in the hymns in Luke 1 and 2, and in Rev. 19.

That little word "for" takes an important role also in Isa. 43:1-7, the stated text for the first Sunday in the New Year in cycle C. But in that passage the repetitions are very important too. Look at that passage.

"Created" and "formed" (vv. 1, 7). The passage is addressed to a people created by God, but according to verse 7, a people also called by His name. That certainly applies to the church. The church has been created, formed by God, and every baptized soul is called by His name. We are all "Christians," "Christ's people," so we can take the passage as a text directed to us.

There are two important repetitions: "Fear not" (vv. 1, 5) and "I am with you" (vv. 2, 5). These are two great notes sounding forth from the Lord from the reaches of heaven.

"For" also comes into prominence here and gives the reasons why we should not fear. The English translations don't show this, but in the Hebrew, "for" begins five different phrases, all explaining the reason why we should not fear in our situations:

- v. 1—"fear not, for I have redeemed you" (from sin and death by the Cross and Resurrection)
- v. 2—fear not, for "when you pass through the waters . . . they shall not overwhelm you" (symbol of darkness, evil, death); fear not, for "when you walk through fire [the fires of testing] you shall not be burned"
- v. 3—fear not, "for I am the LORD your God" (and that echoes the covenant relation in Christ)
- v. 5—"fear not, for I am with you" (which we know from the promise of Christ that He is with us always) (By that structure we are given the content of the sermon that tells our people why they need not fear.) (all RSV)

In watching for the little word "for," it's also important to realize that it never should be divided from the sentence that precedes it. For example, the New Testament uses Matt. 20:1 as the beginning of a new chapter. But the verse begins with "for" and so it should not be separated from 19:30, and the repetition of 19:30 in 20:16 confirms that. In the same manner, "for" does not mark the beginning of a stanza in the Bible's poetry, despite the stanza divisions in English translations, and those divisions can be all-important in grasping the meaning of a text.

Adversatives in the Bible are also exceedingly important. For example, Joel 2:12-17 is always the stated Old Testament text for Ash Wednesday in the three-year lectionary. That prophet announces the coming of the Day of the Lord, the day of God's final judgment on all of us. But despite that judgment, verse 12 begins with that wonderful adversative, "Yet even now"—even now in all of our sinfulness, even now in our situation, even now no matter what our condition, God offers a return to Him, because He is gracious and merciful, slow to anger, and abounding in steadfast love. What a message of mercy—God's great reversal, God's "nevertheless," God's contradicting word, shown forth in those adversatives in the Scriptures. Other examples may be noted. When the women went to the tomb to anoint Jesus' body, "they found the stone rolled away from the tomb, *but* when they went in they did not find the body" (Luke 24:2-3, RSV, emphasis added). "All flesh is grass, and all its beauty is like the flower of the field. . . . The grass withers, the flowers fade; *but* the word of our God will stand for ever" (Isa. 40:6, 8, RSV, emphasis added).

If we carefully note all of these rhetorical structures in the text, we immerse ourselves in the text, and we are much less likely to preach our own thoughts instead of those of the Scriptures.

In analyzing a biblical text, the immediate context is also important. The well-known lines in Mic. 6:8 belong with what goes before in verses 1-7, which has the form of a court case. God presents His case in verses 1-5, and His charge is that His people say He has "wearied" them (v. 3). Israel replies to that in verses 6-7, and the question is, How are Israel's words in verses 6-7 to be interpreted? Is Israel still "wearied" with the Lord? Are the questions in verses 6-7 spoken in weariness or in the sarcasm that believes that nothing will satisfy the Lord? I, along with Luther, believe it is the latter interpretation. But to that weary sarcasm the Lord then replies in verse 8, in the great patience of His mercy.

The cross-references of a biblical text are also important—those listed in a center-column or footnoted cross-referenced Bible. If the preacher will take the time and trouble to pursue those references or search a concordance for the same words, that exercise can be an enormous help in understanding both how the Scriptures have interpreted a passage ("scriptures interpret scriptures")—and in finding how the passage forms a trajectory through the sacred history.

Note this example. In the court case of Jer. 2:4-13, the stated text for Proper 17 in Year C of the lectionary, the Lord describes himself as "the fountain of living waters" in verse 13. He accuses Israel in the same verse of rejecting God's never-failing waters of life in order to dig for herself worthless cisterns in the desert—cisterns that can hold no water. How does that square with what we find in the New Testament? Well, we don't find the phrase "living waters" in a concordance, but if we look up the word "living," we are directed to John 4:10-14. There Jesus tells the Samaritan woman that He can provide "living water"—"a spring of water welling up to eternal life." Similarly, in John 8:38, the Lord speaks of "living water" flowing out of the heart of anyone who comes to him. The pairing of the Old Testament texts thus gives the immediate indication of where, like Israel, a congregation may find the waters of eternal life. The preacher can therefore illumine Israel's situation in the time of Jeremiah in the late seventh century B.C., when Israel is going after all of those false gods, the "worthless cisterns," and then show how that is also the story of our modern lives in Jesus Christ.

All of this digging into a biblical passage, analyzing its structure and examining its context, and tracing its trajectory insures almost inevitably, if the work is carefully and faithfully done, that the preacher will preach from the biblical text and not from his or her own opinion or view. What happens in the process is that God, if He so wills by His Spirit, uses the text to work His work and speak His Word to the church. Then our preaching indeed becomes sacramental. Then it does become the word and action of the living God—of that magnificent God who transforms human lives, who makes all things new, and who, in His love, moves steadily forward toward His good and joyful kingdom here on our earth.

William Willimon, S.T.D., has been dean of the Chapel and professor of Christian ministry at Duke University in Durham, North Carolina, since 1984. He has served as pastor of churches in Georgia and South Carolina. In 1996, an international survey conducted by Baylor University named him 1 of the 12 most effective preachers in the English-speaking world. He is the author of 50 books. His articles have appeared in many publications including *The Christian Ministry, Worship,* and *Christianity Today.* His *Pulpit Resource* is used each week by over 8,000 pastors in the U.S.A., Canada, and Australia. He serves on the editorial boards of *The Christian Century, The Christian Ministry, Pulpit Digest, Preaching, The Wittenburg Door,* and *Leadership.* He has given lectures and taught courses at many pastors' schools, colleges, and universities in the United States, Canada, Europe, and Asia. He is married to Patricia Parker. The Willimons have two children: William Parker and Harriet Patricia.

7

Preaching as Worship

William Willimon

❧ AS THE PEOPLE OFFER UP THEIR MONEY, PRAYERS, BREAD AND WINE, hopes and fears, doubts and praise, they ask the pastor to offer a sermon. The sermon is the preacher's service. It is service that is sometimes a gift: the gift of healing, sustaining, guiding, encouraging the people. It is also service that is sometimes a burden: the burden of witnessing to the truth, speaking like a prophet, saying the things that are not pleasant to hear.

But whether it is experienced on any given Sunday as a burden or as a blessing, the sermon is always an act of worship. As John Knox says,

> Unless we conceive of preaching as being itself an act of worship, we miss what is most essential in it and what distinguishes it most radically from other kinds of teaching, religious or secular. The real truth of the matter is not that preaching merely happens usually to be set in a context of worship or that it is most effective when it has that kind of setting. Rather, it cannot be really preaching except in that context. If the context of worship is not there already, the true sermon creates it. Either preaching contributes to, provides a medium of worship, or it is not preaching at all.
>
> Knox sees the liturgical character of a sermon most clearly in the preparation of the sermon. A sermon should be prepared, he says, as an act of worship, the offering of the preacher, a prayer.
>
> The sermon is an offering to God—or rather it is the preacher offering himself to God—and the preparation is a disciplined act of devotion. To preach is really to pray with others, to lead others in prayer; to prepare to preach is, certainly under one important aspect, to pray for others and for oneself for the sake of others.[1]

Understanding the sermon as an act of worship has far-reaching consequences related to the nature of worship. Christian worship has its primary focus in the praise and adoration of God; all other activity is secondary to our response to a loving Creator. Worship has no more worthy purpose than the proclamation, praise, and adoration of God. Whenever worship is *used* for some other purpose—worthy though it may be—it is being used and thereby *abused.* The focus of worship is God, not us. Whenever we use worship to educate, titillate, soothe, anger, instruct, judge, or do other things to people, the primary focus of worship has shifted from God to us. Utilitarianism—the limited, anthropocentric point of view that regards all experiences, feelings, and thoughts on the basis of human utility is the very antithesis of Christian worship. It's not about us. It's about God.

This is not to say that worship has no human consequences. While we are praising God, we often find that something happens to us. Sometimes, we are educated, titillated, soothed, angered, instructed, or judged. But all these come as a result of focusing our affections upon God, as a gracious by-product of worship. The main thing that happens to us in worship and the primary reason we keep doing it is that we are brought close to God.

Some of us who orchestrate and concoct services of worship that are designed on the basis of how effectively they move the congregation from point A to point B need to ask ourselves, Who is worship for, anyway? Whenever we are the center of our worship, the final test for its faithfulness, or the goal toward which all its activity moves we are doing something other than worshiping God.

What does this mean for preaching? I find it helpful to think of sermons, in their various forms, as various acts of worship. Some sermons are doxologies—because there is truth that is preached best by being sung. Some sermons are prayers—because the preacher is speaking as much of *our* needs as of his or her needs. Some are like the Lord's Supper —because the preacher is but one hungry person telling other hungry persons where to find bread. Some are pure credo—bold affirmation of the truth we hold and the truth that holds us. All sermons are oblation —offering what we have before God who takes it, blesses it, and gives it to feed the hungry multitudes.

Thinking of the sermon as an act of worship has some immediate practical consequences. For one thing, it reminds us that a sermon is as much something that we *do* as something we *say.* Contemporary worship renewal has noted that worship is more a series of actions than a set of words. In the centuries after the Reformation many churches fell into worship patterns that were mostly words: the pastor's duty was mostly to speak and the congregation's duty was mostly to listen. Prayer books, printed bulletins, and hymnals—all inventions made possible by the Gutenberg printing revolution—reinforced the notion that words were more important in worship than deeds.

Now we are learning again to trust the power of the symbolic, the efficacy of the visual. We are learning again the joy of focusing our attention upon the ordinary stuff of everyday life and seeing God revealed in it—in the bread and wine, the water, a handshake, an embrace. Many of us worship leaders, therefore, are having to correct old habits. Presiding in the liturgy requires sensitivity to body language—what we say by how we do things.

As a teacher of preaching in a seminary, I would have to say that my students find it most difficult to conceive of the sermon as (like most acts of worship) a visual as well as an auditory experience. Our sermons must be prepared not only by paying attention to what we say but also by paying attention to how we say it. A mirror or video recorder can be as helpful here as a lectionary and commentary. Honest observers who carefully watch how we do things in our preaching and then tell us what they see can also be helpful. We do little good if we speak of grace and then appear to be ungracious in the way we invite persons to the Communion table or hand them bread or greet them at the end of the worship.

For some time now homiletics professors have criticized the oratorical, rhetorical style of preaching of the past. Bombastic oratory is probably inappropriate for most Christian communication. One has to admit, however, that many preachers of a bygone era were sensitive to the visual aspects of public speaking in a way that we are not.

Read Spurgeon's *Lectures to My Students* and note the detailed instructions he gives for body gestures. A minister who drools into the microphone, hides behind the pulpit, mumbles and slurs words, or slouches at the altar cheapens the message. We do not put our hands in our pockets when we say something important. We do not shout and flail our arms in the air when we offer consolation. As one person said of her pastor, "He has no sense of occasion. His sermons are all warm fireside chats at which he smiles and talks softly—regardless of the text, the season, or the occasion. This is as inappropriate as if he screamed at us in every sermon." Our gestures, movement, posture, and facial expression should be appropriate. Though it pains me somewhat as a preacher to admit this, actions do speak louder than words.

Using intentional, firm, confident gestures helps make the congregation comfortable because then persons know someone is in charge who feels good about leading them. Attractive, neat, and colorful vestments help set the tone for the assembly.

But a pastor's eyes are the principal means of communicating with and leading the congregation. When the choir sings, therefore, the leader's eyes should be on them. When a lay reader is reading the scripture, the pastor's eyes should be on that person. When the pastor gives bread to a person in the Lord's Supper, he or she should establish eye contact and hold it while placing the bread in the communicant's hand. During periods of silence (all too infrequent in most of our services) the minister can help the congregation focus inwardly by focusing his or her eyes, settling into a comfortable but not slouching posture, and using the silence for real reflection. All these gestures help proclaim the gospel as vividly and pointedly as any words we may speak. The sermon is an act of worship.

We can also avoid a host of homiletical sins by preparing the sermons as if we were preparing a liturgical activity. Some time ago one of my evangelical friends said, "All preaching must lead to response." But if all preaching is designed to elicit some kind of concrete human response, then it cannot always be biblical preaching (unless we define *response* so broadly that the word loses its meaning). Numerous portions of Scripture do not call for a response—except a loud amen! For example, what kind of response does this passage evoke: "O the depth of the riches and wisdom and knowledge of God! How unsearchable are his judgments and how inscrutable his ways!" (Rom. 11:33, NRSV)?

Much biblical truth is meant simply to be affirmed as true, to be adored rather than acted upon. Much of it is truth about who God is rather than what we are to do. It is truth that, as in any act of worship, is to be sung, shouted, adored, or quietly reflected upon. When preaching on this kind of truth, the preacher simply proclaims reality: the way things are, what God has done and is doing.

Certainly such truth has ethical implications. A song, a poem, an hour of quiet meditation, a vision of reality—even the impact of a pastor's personality—may lead to changed lives, courageous action, or heroic commitment. But such response comes as response to the truth, to our vision of the way things are in this world now that God has gotten into the act. Worship is mainly responsive, reflexive, and much good preaching out to be that way too. It's about God.

One of the most difficult things in worship is for the leader to lead without getting in the way, so to speak. In our protest against some of the inhuman, robot-like liturgical leadership of the past, some of us overreact. We turn worship into a folksy, preacher-orchestrated hour in which the congregation is treated to the innermost thoughts and aspirations of the pastor or to jokes or to warm moments or to prophetic ravings—depending on the pastor's personality and theological inclinations. Sometimes people complain that they cannot see God for looking at the pastor!

Ours is a difficult task in preaching or in worship leadership: to convey sensitivity, warmth, and care in our liturgical leadership and still provide a setting whereby worshipers are enabled to see through us to God. Only a thin line separates the facilitating of congregational worship from becoming the center of worship. Sometimes we do not know when we do overstep that line; then an honest friend can help us evaluate our public worship-leadership style.

I like to use the analogy of a chairperson at a meeting. The best chairpersons move us along to our common goal without obstructing our movement by taking over the meeting. Their main function is to call the group's attention to what needs to be done, help the group listen to itself, then move the meeting to its conclusion. They trust the group and its resources. When our sermons center on "The Life and Struggles of Pastor X," we are in danger of turning the sermons into performances rather than oblations. The history of worship warns us against the human tendency to make worship into a drama to be observed and admired by the faithful: the faith is always to be lived, not merely watched. When we see the sermon as a tool to get people to do this or that no matter how beneficial to them or the church—proclamation has degenerated into manipulation and the worship of God into a technique for merely entertaining people. Then the sermon attends, not to the mystery of God, but to the self-evident, the trite, the didactic. It lapses into humanistic platitudes and simplistic solutions for the human plight, and boredom is the inevitable result.

Trusting the Word and trusting persons to hear and respond to the Word in their own way are part of a basic respect for persons and for the Word of God that enables worship to take place.

Like any good liturgy, thoughtful sermons are an invitation to risk meeting and being met by God—no matter what the consequences. We cannot force that meeting in liturgy or in preaching. We cannot determine in advance what the consequences of such a meeting will be. We can only call persons to the meeting, help focus their attention, set the context in which the meeting may happen, and give participants space to follow the Spirit. This is the goal in planning preaching or worship.

WORSHIP AS THE SETTING FOR THE SERMON

We have said that the sermon is an act of worship and the gospel is proclaimed in both word and deed. At one time we Protestants saw the sermon as *the* act of worship; all else in the service was a preliminary to the preaching. But now new understandings of the purpose of Sunday morning have brought things into better balance. Word *and* the sacrament are the two historic foci for Sunday worship.

I think of the relationship between the sermon and the Lord's Supper this way: The Eucharist is primarily an eschatological, ecstatic experience. It provides a time apart. The meal is a foretaste of the banquet in the Kingdom. In this time of eating and drinking with Christ, our eyes are opened and we see the hungry multitudes coming and being filled, we see sinners at the gospel feast, we welcome these strangers as brothers and sisters in Christ. The presence of the risen Christ is made real, and we glimpse the promised new heaven and new earth (see Rev. 21:1).

All this can and often does happen when we celebrate the Lord's Supper. It is therefore a joyous, healing, resurrection occasion. But in the midst of this joy and thanksgiving for God's victory in Christ, the sermon says, "Yes—but not yet."

The sermon is therefore a contemporaneous reminder that we still live between the times, stretched between the now of life in this world and the not-yet of God's complete redemption of the world. The decisive victory has been won, but many battles remain to be fought. The sermon often speaks of those battles. It points to the reality of a creation that still groans in travail as it awaits redemption. It speaks of the Monday-morning blues, of cornflakes at breakfast, of the cancer that will not heal, of the marriage that will not last, and of the oppression that goes on and on. The sermon is bitingly, pointedly, specifically contemporary in the midst of our Eucharistic remembrance and foretaste. It reminds us that we are brothers and sisters in Christ—but not yet. We are redeemed —but not yet. God rules over all—but not yet. The hungry are being filled with good things—but not yet.

Without a good, cold dose of the preached Word, therefore, our Sunday worship can become a detached fantasy trip that is more an escape from the truth of God than an encounter with that truth. Paul had to tell the Corinthians (1 Cor. 11—12) that their lack of love had made their worship a mockery. Paul's homiletical realism is a much-needed corrective for any church that prematurely announces the advent of the Kingdom in its gatherings.

On the other hand, sermons detached from worship threaten to overwhelm the congregation by listing human failures without celebrating God's victory. Without the sacramental, eschatological vision the sermon tends always to say, "No, no, not yet." The word is spoken but not enacted. The vision is sketched, sometimes in vivid words, but never embodied in bread and wine. The presence of the risen Christ is pointed to but never touched.

Prophetic or judgmental sermons leave the congregation to wallow in the mire of all the things it is not, rather than moving on to celebrate who, by God's grace, it is. And affirming and encouraging sermons frustrate the congregation because it is never able to act upon what it feels: an invitation to the feast is given but the feast is left uneaten.

How those of us who are heirs of the evangelical tradition could forget that the sermon is an invitation to the gospel feast is one of the most distressing mysteries of church history. Yet with my free-church heritage, I can still affirm that the sermon is at the center of Sunday morning worship, for it can be at the center without being the climax. The reading and preaching of God's Word can be the central point toward which the first acts of worship move and from which later acts flow.

This centrality is mainly a structural matter. When planning our pattern of worship, we need to ask, What do we need to do to gather to hear God's Word? Worship planners are taking seriously the need for a time of gathering in the service. Informal and formal greetings, welcome of visitors, announcements, rehearsal of new music—all are appropriate activities during the gathering. From the gathering, all hymns, prayers, and responses before the scripture reading and the sermon should be seen as _preparation_ for hearing. Such gathering and preparation assume that we need to prepare our congregation's own individual hearts and minds for the word. None of us knows how many sermons fall on deaf ears for lack of adequate congregational participation.

Likewise, all acts that follow the reading and preaching can be seen as fitting responses to the word. For many of us this means planning more acts of worship to come after the sermon. A creed, the offering, prayers of thanksgiving and intercession, baptism, and the Lord's Supper are best seen as response to the word. As we noted earlier, most of our services lack sufficient opportunity for a variety of congregational response. The word seems to fall on deaf ears. We preach the word—but then we do nothing. Rising to our feet after the sermon with a hearty "This we believe . . . ," coming forward for baptism or for the Lord's Supper, and praying for the needs of the world are most effective as postsermon responses. In this way our liturgy becomes a symbol for the way we experience the Christian life inside and outside the church: hearing the word, being touched by the truth, then responding to that revelation in word and deed. When this happens, liturgy is life, the word becomes flesh in our lives, and the integration that is at the heart of faith itself occurs.

You open the Bible and begin to read, wondering through the words that flow from the text what will happen to your words. What good will this do? What harm will it do? Whose life will it affect? What demons will be set in motion once the word is turned loose in their hearts? What will happen to you—or in you?

All that is left is for you to speak. And for the hundredth time, in spite of all the questions that have no answers, in spite of all the misgivings, the doubts, the lack of answers, you do speak. For the hundredth Sunday you take all those feelings, doubts, questions, all the confusion, the unknowing, and the faith—you lay them all upon the altar, before God and everyone else. You know this is not the best sermon that could be preached, but it is the only one you have today. You know you cannot say all that could be said, but it is all that will be said here today. You know you are not the best of preachers, but you are the best your congregation has now.

So you speak. You never cease to be amazed that you have the courage to speak. You wonder how you have the nerve to do it. But your flock have offered themselves, given God what they have—so now you give what you have. You take it all and lay it upon the altar as your gift, your offering, your oblation. You dare to speak. You dare to lay your offering before them. And because you do, the word is let loose, the Spirit starts to rove among them, for better or worse, the gospel feast begins again. For the millionth time in our story, God's people hear the word, and they are fed.

Notes

1. John Knox, *The Integrity of Preaching* (Nashville: Abingdon Press, 1957), 76. For a full treatment of preaching as a liturgical activity, see William Skudlarek, *The Word in Worship: Preaching in a Liturgical Context* (Nashville: Abingdon, 1981).

This chapter is adapted from William H. Willimon, *Integrative Preaching: the Pulpit at the Center*, chap. 6 (Nashville: Abingdon, 1981).

Darius Salter is currently professor of Christian preaching and pastoral theology at Nazarene Theological Seminary in Kansas City. For eight years he served as chairman of the Pastoral Studies Department at Western Evangelical Seminary in Portland, Oregon. He was the executive director of the Christian Holiness Association, an interdenominational fellowship consisting of 17 denominations, 50 colleges and universities, and two missionary organizations, from 1979 to 1986. Dr. Salter directed the Doctor of Ministry program at Nazarene Theological Seminary from 1991 to1996, and the Supervised Ministries program from 1991 to 2001.

As a pastor, Dr. Salter was senior pastor at First Friends Church, Canton, Ohio, 1976-79, and before that an ordained deacon in the United Methodist Church in which he pastored for six years. Dr. Salter was ordained an elder in the Church of the Nazarene in 1988.

Dr. Salter's educational background includes the M.Div. from Asbury Theological Seminary and the Ph.D. from Drew University. He is the author of several books: *Spirit and Intellect: Thomas Upham's Holiness Theology, What Really Matters in Ministry: Profiling Pastoral Success in Flourishing Churches, American Evangelism: Its Theology and Practice,* and *Prophetical-Priestly Words: Biblical Identity for the 21st Century Pastor.* His latest book is a critical biography of Francis Asbury titled *America's Bishop: The Life of Francis Asbury.*

Dr. Salter is married to Brenda, and they have four daughters: Heather, Heidi, Tabitha, and Ashley. The Salters reside in Lake Winnebago, Missouri.

8

Preaching as God Encounter

Darius Salter

ALL SCRIPTURE IS ABOUT GOD. AND SINCE ALL SERMONS SHOULD be an exposition of scripture (I use the word *exposition* for a wide variety of forms), they should be about God. Granted, the "God sense" of some scripture is much more explicit than that of others. A historical statement in the Old Testament such as 2 Kings 15:1-2, which states that Azariah was 16 years old when he became king and ruled for 52 years, does not deserve to be chosen as a biblical text—especially if some wild allegorization or numerical theologizing were implemented. Certainly something could be said about God's superintending historical events! The preacher, however, must periodically take to heart the adage of Sigmund Freud that "sometimes a cigar is only a cigar."

For any portion of scripture that assumes the stature of a sermonic text, the preacher must assess what God is doing in it. All worthwhile preaching identifies the "God role" in human existence. I designate this God role as the theology of the text. Theology for the purpose of preaching is describing and defining how God views our existence. And as I repeatedly remind my students, the theology of preaching is simple, nontechnical, and mostly monosyllabic: "life is short, eternity is long, God is love, Christ is alive, grace is free, sin is destructive, things are fleeting, hope is real, and relationships are important." If preaching is "God encounter," those themes as well as others will be repeated ad infinitum. God encounter frees parishioners from the apparent goods of life to the real goods of life. God encounter preempts the world's definition of blessedness with God's definition of blessedness.

Paul Scott Wilson indicts preachers for not stopping "to ensure that out of their biblical text, they make claims about who God is, or what God has done, is doing, and has promised to do."[1] The optimum question of any text or any sermon is, "What is uttered about God?"[2] The task of all preaching is getting God right. "The God who is revealed through Scripture is legitimately sought in Scripture and the biblical text's answer to *Who is God? What is God saying? What is God doing?* is a way at arriving at a legitimate literal sense, a highly literal sense of the biblical text when it is read as Scripture."[3]

Allow me to demonstrate "God encounter" with two passages found in the New Testament. Both can be interpreted in at least two alternate ways. John 21 narrates one of the post-Resurrection appearances of Christ to His disciples. These disciples have fished all night and have caught nothing. Jesus says to them, "Cast the net on the right-hand side of the boat, and you will find a catch." The disciples obeyed Christ and "they were not able to haul it in because of the great number of fish" (v. 6, NASB). Some preachers may choose to emphasize the willingness of the disciples to try something different. Certainly both pastors and churches often fail to recognize the rut and continue to do things as "they have always done them before." Another sermon on the passage may contain the proposition that faith and obedience are handmaidens and the disciples demonstrated both by their compliance to Jesus' command. After all, what would a carpenter know about fishing?

Both of the above are ideas in this text and merit mention within the sermon, but I believe neither are the dominant idea. I choose to focus on the supernatural intervention of God in the mundane activities of life. Let's face it, life is full of the routine. In Dorothy Sayers' words, "The problem with life is that it is so everlastingly daily." Or for the commercial fisherman, "so everlastingly nightly." We do the same thing over and over again. The truth of the text is that the disciples did not cast their nets in a different place. They dropped it where they had in all probability just let it down. The place is the same whether one puts the net out on the left side or the right side of the boat.

How often have we stood in the same pulpit and preached Sunday after Sunday? The paucity of the results or the ineptitude of our performance did not prevent us from preaching again the next Sunday. In spite of our futile attempts at telling the "greatest story ever told" as it ought to be, we do it over and over again. But we should never preach with less than the expectation that this sermon will be something different. We should never preach with less than the expectation that God will break in on this one occasion to such an extent that this worship service and this sermon will be forever remembered by those who were there that day. No fisherman would forget the morning he caught 153 fish, so many that the boat was not large enough to hold them. He would tell about it for the rest of his life.

A very perplexing event in the life of Christ is the "cursing of the fig tree" (Matt. 21:18-22 and Mark 11:12-14). This is the only time Scripture records Christ using miraculous power for destructive purposes. In fact, the event seems so incongruent with the life of Christ that some scholars say it did not happen. Some biblical exegetes suggest that the writer has concocted a story from the parable of the fig tree told by Jesus. In other words, the operative hermeneutic is that if a scripture passage does not fit in my "God box," if it is not in keeping with my view of God, then dismiss it. But for me and, I believe, many others, the confounding nature of this event makes it that much more intriguing. Since the cursing of the fig tree is coupled with Jesus' cleansing of the Temple, one might choose to stress Israel's barren spiritual existence and apply the event to the fruitless existence of some of today's churches. This idea is intrinsic to the text, but in my perception is not the dominant idea in it.

The clue to this text is provided by close examination of the fig tree. This fig tree is alone, an accident, not in a grove of fig trees, not encouraged by other fig trees, with roots in arid, sandy soil on the side of a hill, battered by wind, cold, heat, and parasites. (Look how good the olive trees have it.) There is no evidence that this tree was ever nurtured, cultivated, or fertilized. The circumstances of the tree predestined it to a barren death. Then comes the clincher, "It was not the season for figs." Instead of cursing the tree, why didn't Jesus hang an "out of season" sign on it?" Anyone should have known that on this particular day, it was impossible for this tree to yield fruit. Which is precisely the point, "God expects the impossible."

I am always capable of discovering circumstances (excuses) to explain why my life is barren. But the bearing of fruit is not predicated on circumstances. Fruit is produced because my life is deeply rooted in God's grace. I can always articulate reasons (excuses) why my life is "out of season." But in the light of God's power and promises, life is always "in season." When I stand before God for His final assessment, whatever I say better not be, "But, God, you don't understand, it was out of season." The good news of the cursing of the fig tree is the unqualified promise of Jesus, whatever the circumstances, "I am the vine, you are the branches; he who abides in Me, and I in him, he bears much fruit; for apart from Me you can do nothing" (John 15:5, NASB).

Some may accuse me of arbitrariness in choosing the dominant idea of the text, which in turn becomes the key point in the sermon. I do not deny bringing a theological matrix to the text. The issue is not whether or not I am guilty of eisegesis; the critical question ought to be: "Is my eisegesis in continuity with the tenor of Scripture?" Over the years I have developed a theological grid that among other convictions consists of a God who bestows abundant grace upon His creation and desires for every person to develop his or her full potential in Jesus Christ. In other words, the theme of the biblical story is redemption. I bring redemption to every text and use it as the linchpin for every sermon. Biblical warnings about an eternity without God are for the purpose of redemption. Overall biblical perspective provides theological consistency and continuity for every sermon we preach. The Bible is primarily about what God does, and, secondarily, about what humans do. Good preaching is God-centered (Christ-centered) rather than human-centered.

Optimum questions for any sermon are, "Who is God?" "What is God doing?" and "What does God provide?" Paul Wilson defines the "God sense" of the scripture as "those dimensions of it that speak of God's nature, acts, and relationships to humanity and creation, and that enable the Bible to be read as Scripture, the book of the church."[4] The clue to making God the creative power of every sermon is paying close attention to how God reveals himself in Scripture. God majors in communication. Allow me to highlight at least three of His methodologies.

A. GRAPHIC SPEECH

Attentive Bible reading is synonymous with a course in graphic arts. God employs cinematography rather than how-to manuals. All sermon preparation requires three-dimensional glasses that transpose flat-line images into hurling objects. At least once in a while, both preacher and people need to feel like ducking, rather than politely listening. The Bible does not proposition its auditors; it shocks, scares, arrests, and awakens them with smoke, fire, stones, swords, brides, prostitutes, gardens, gates, snakes, and bones. These images allow sermons to become love affairs, battlefields, and courtroom dramas. Abraham Heschel states that God's images "must not shine, they must burn."[5]

In Luke 22:29, Jesus states to His disciples, "Just as my father gave to me a Kingdom, I give a kingdom to you" (author's translation). A short while later, the crowd who gathered at Pilate's judgment hall (what would that look like on a movie set?) would choose between two kingdoms. Would they choose the lowly Nazarene or the insurrectionist and murderer, Barabbas? I want my listeners to see, smell, and hear Barabbas. Barabbas reeks of body odor, glistens with sweat, snarls with obscenities, and foams at the mouth. This barbaric savage is unshaven, filthy, and bulging with muscles, which are restrained by chains and manacles. After describing Barabbas, I return to Jesus' declaration of the Kingdom gift. What kind of domain was Jesus offering? A four-bedroom house on a corner lot? Employment with fringe benefits and a good retirement plan?

Before I answer the above, I return to Barabbas, whom we have typecast and miscast. I believe that we would need to choose Sean Connery to play Barabbas, the original 007: "My name is Bond, James Bond." Barabbas was chisel-faced, steel-eyed, square-jawed, and dapperly draped in an Armani suit. As an insurrectionist, he was a champion of the people, an avenger of justice, and the hope of the enslaved Jews to free them from the Roman government. Barabbas had much to offer: profit-sharing, linear security, and entitlement to one's fair share of the Israeli (American) pie. All Jesus has to offer is the cross. The fringe benefits are not all that inviting. The choice the crowd made that day between two kingdoms clues me in on the kind of kingdom Jesus was offering His disciples, the same kingdom that He offers you and me: "You can have all of the turf you want, as long as its boundaries are defined by the cross."

Jeremiah earned an A for sermon illustration. His illustrations were a tangible, observable acting out of the spoken word. God not only gave the Word but also gave instructions acting it out. "Take the waistband that you have bought . . . and arise, go to the Euphrates and hide it there in a crevice of the rock" (13:4, NASB). "Arise and go down to the potter's house, and there I shall announce My words to you" (18:2, NASB). "Go and buy a potter's earthenware jar" (19:1, NASB). "The LORD showed me: behold, two baskets of figs set before the temple of the LORD" (24:1, NASB). "Buy for yourself my field which is at Anathoth, for you have the right of redemption to buy it" (32:7, NASB). "Go to the house of the Rechabites and speak to them, and bring them into the house of the LORD, into one of the chambers, and give them wine to drink" (35:2, NASB). All of these tendentious activities addressed God's relationship with Judah—His holy faithfulness that would carry out His righteous justice as opposed to Judah's stubborn self-sovereignty. It would get worse before it got better.

God contextualizes communication. It behooves His messengers to do the same. Words are vessels; the vessels change as the communication context changes. It is not only that a pottery illustration may not hold the attention of a suburban congregation, but that my pottery craftsmanship or lack thereof would only demonstrate that God is making a mess of things. Sermons must be within the media matrix that is most meaningful. That does not mean we are to substitute cinematography for a Spirit-filled sermon embodied and proclaimed via a Spirit-anointed personality. But it perhaps does mean that our sermons need to be Spirit-anointed cinematography. Preaching that consists simply of syllogistic logic and propositional persuasion will increasingly fall on the deaf ears of postmoderns. If the Enlightenment has run out of fuel, then pulpit communication will need to be more of a visual, imaginative encounter than a rational construct. Sermons will consist of plots, scenes, and characters with which auditors can identify because there is a mutuality of plight and solution.

The Bible is a story offering a flood of light on the human predicament. This spotlight leaves all of us found out, if not by others, at least by God. The biblical floodlight is not for the purpose of stripping us for full disclosure by onlookers, but for us to be able to perceive ourselves within the flow of God's transforming grace. Scripture is the story of God's offer of grace to the greedy, lustful, deceitful, proud, immoral, and anxious—in other words, to us. Though the context of life is different, the essential character is the same. Jacob is everyman and Mary Magdalene is everywoman.

The story deserves to be told well. Some of the telling comes naturally because it is a universal trait to tell and to listen to stories. Walter Fisher argues that the universal trait of storytelling means "that symbols are created and communicated ultimately as stories meant to give order to human experience and to induce others to dwell in them in order to establish ways of living in common, in intellectual and spiritual communities in which there is confirmation for the story that constitutes one's life."[6] Words are images. Sermons will have to become "imagologies." In Mark Taylor's words, "Imagology insists that the word is never simply a word, but is always also an image."[7] Imagology overcomes spatial limitations by transcending centuries and traversing the globe.

When sermons become imagologies, they enter into cyberspace, becoming accessible to people of all ages and all places. But they do not carry the sanitized, abstract, detached quality of cyberspace. Preaching is injected with sights, sounds, feelings, and attitudes that catch the attention of the archetypical formation that is a part of every consciousness or unconsciousness. These images elicit latent emotions, reveal enslaving attitudes, expose crippling scars, and above all inspire hope. Rahab is the "mole on the wall who made it to the hall." Judah is the horny father-in-law who fathered two illegitimate children by his daughter-in-law, thus providing a direct genetic link to Christ. Soap operas were a reality before there was soap—at least soap commercials.

There was once a pastor whose suburban church yawned instead of "amened" and prided themselves on being included rather than busying themselves on the activity of inclusion. One day God spoke to the pastor, "Go marry a whore." Boy, did the church wake up when this pastor brought his red-light district prize to introduce her to the congregation! As he introduced her to the astonished parishioners, he announced that their gift registry was at Bloomenstiens. The honor and the sanctity of the church had been desecrated. Hosea finally had gotten the church's attention. The church made news. They had a pastor married to a prostitute. In fact, he had been married to a prostitute all along—them.

Israel had committed whoredom. She had been lulled into complacency by the allurement of false gods whom she sought out of selfish interests. The union with false gods out of impulsive lusts gave birth to children. The children were named "Delayed Damnation," "No More Mercy," and "Illegitimate." They were a not-so-happy family. Of course they had been unhappy all along, but up until now the root causes of their unhappiness had not been so graphically illustrated. Dysfunctionalism was as bad as it gets. The mom took to the streets again. Not much psychological hope exists for children who hear the taunts of their classmates, "Your mother is a whore." The plot is full of anger, lust, greed, guilt, sorrow, and the desperate need for redemption. Just like life. Just like the people in our churches. Just like those our sermons need to describe and feel and image.

We have the events and the emotions, but we lack scriptwriters, people with imagination, people who can readdress the biblical drama in a contemporary idiom. There probably never has been a better scriptwriter than Robert G. Lee, pastor of the Bellevue Baptist Church in Memphis. Note his description of Jezebel, who laid the plot for her husband to kill Naboth, owner of a coveted vineyard.

> Hear her derisive laugh as it rings out in the palace like the shrill crackle of a wild owl that has returned to its nest and has found a serpent therein! With her tongue, sharp as a razor, she prods Ahab as an ox driver prods with sharp goad the ox which does not want to press his neck into the yoke, or as one whips with a rawhide a stubborn mule. With profuse and harsh laughter this old gay gaudy guinea of Satan derided this king of hers for a cowardly buffoon and sordid jester. What hornet-like sting in her sarcasm! What wolf-mouth taunts she hurled at him for his scrupulous timidity! Her bosom with anger was heaving! Her eyes were flashing with rage under the surge of hot anger that swept over her.[8]

For Robert G. Lee and those who heard him, the sermon was not only something to be heard but also something to be seen and felt. The camera had zeroed in on jealousy personified in all of its grotesque manifestations. Certainly we would not want to live with her, which is precisely the point. Then "Why do we?" is the apt question. But the question deserves to be asked only if the script has sufficiently completed its task. If not, we are only left with a moralism. "Don't be jealous." Such sermons never work.

But the question deserves to be asked, "Must every sermon be a grotesque caricature of the sordid traits of life? Do we have to follow the present trend of cinematography, that is, blood and guts to attract viewers (listeners)? Does every sermon have to be a narrative about murder, theft, and God's revenge?" The staple, if not overwhelming, may become a bit tiring. Hopefully all cinematography does not have to go the way of Jezebel's demise. "These men put their strong men's fingers into her soft feminine flesh and picked her up, tired head and all, painted face and all, bejeweled fingers and all—and threw her down. Her body hit the street and burst open."[9]

Note the correlating scene from Jeremiah, "Then I will make to cease from the cities of Judah and from the streets of Jerusalem the voice of joy and the voice of gladness, the voice of the bridegroom and the voice of the bride; for the land will become a ruin" (7:34, NASB). The phrase "voice of the bridegroom and the voice of the bride" is unique to Jeremiah. He uses the phrase four times: 7:34; 16:9; 25:10; 33:11. The scene is of newlyweds. There is vibrancy in their speech, mirth in their words, excitement in their body language, radiance in their countenances, and sheer enjoyment over the presence of the other. The honeymoon is still on. The encounter is both enrapturing and intoxicating. These people are really in love. They really do like each other. Yes, it is idealistic. Most of us have experienced moments of it, animated moments that we hoped would last forever.

But the moments of invigorating reciprocity and mutual devotion did not last forever. The scene has changed. The room is dark and foreboding. The atmosphere is sullen and even bitter. Instead of kindness, there is harshness; instead of a smile, a scowl; instead of affection, animosity. How did we switch scenes? Things became more important than relationships; giving was replaced by getting; lust displaced love; and hurry and worry obscured the good, the beautiful, and the truly rewarding. Vows of trust and fidelity were preempted by cultural mores, distrust, and unfaithfulness. How can we get back? Not easily. Spiteful and abusive spirits are not easy to transform. But there is good news. God can bring healing to the home. "Heal me, O LORD, and I will be healed; save me and I will be saved, for You are my praise" (17:14, NASB).

The characters of cinematography do not consist of propositional constructs but flesh-and-blood persons. The Scriptures introduce traits, attitudes, virtues, ambitions, desires, and sins to us via persons. Most often these persons actually lived, that is, walked planet Earth. At other times, they simply were representative figures, composite profiles who depicted characteristics the speaker desired to highlight. It is an intriguing question, but not crucial whether Jesus actually knew the people of whom He spoke—"a certain rich man and a certain poor man." More importantly, they bear symbolic significance; imaginatively described and highly suggestive of quintessential qualities and particularities that transcend time and space. The whore of Babylon always has been and always will exist, at least until her destruction. Her manifestations are no doubt more alluring in some ages than in others. "For all the nations have drunk of the wine of the passion of her immorality, and the kings of the earth have committed acts of immorality with her, and the merchants of the earth have become rich by the wealth of her sensuality. . . . 'Woe, Woe, the great city, she who was clothed in fine linen and purple and scarlet, and adorned with gold and precious stones and pearls'" (Rev. 18:3, 16, NASB).

Movie cameras never have done justice to Scripture. Its images are so graphic, passionate, and panoramic that representation via celluloid is impossible. The only thing that will work is cinematography via words. As Charles Bartow states in his chapter "Turning Ink into Blood," "Sensory experience is not a plus to thought, it is the stuff of it."[10] Only words can convey and stimulate unlimited imagination. Pictures fail because they are limited by the eye. In contrast, scriptural images are without limit—unlimited sin, unlimited love, and unlimited grace. The pastor prays, "God, don't let my limited, stained-glassed, bland, sanitized, sterilized words limit what you want to do in the human predicament." Jeremiah was not guilty of defining preaching as only polite speech.

B. EMPATHETIC SPEECH

God is anthropathic, that is, He exhibits the same emotions as do humans, or more accurately, we exhibit or should exhibit the same emotions as does God. God's character remains unchanging but His emotions don't. God's emotions are always in keeping with the circumstance of His creation. Had I laughed when I was holding down my two-year-old daughter while a doctor sewed a piece of flesh back into her lip, my emotional state would have been ludicrous. The placid toleration of my wife having an affair would indicate a flaw in both my character and hers. For that reason, lack of passion in preaching is more a theological issue than an emotional one. Dead and dull preaching lacks God's perspective on life. Lack of pathos is a failure to perceive what is at stake when one stands before a congregation of hungering souls. Heschel states, "An analysis of prophetic utterances shows that the fundamental experience of the prophet is a fellowship with the feelings of God, a *sympathy with the divine pathos*, a communion with the divine consciousness which comes about through the prophet's reflection of, or participation in, the divine pathos."[11]

"God perception" elicits "God emotion" in the preacher—love, anger, jealousy, disappointment, and pleasure. Emotions that are trumped up by the preacher are deceitful and manipulative. Emotions that are masked because of false ideas of objectivity or the notion that sermon delivery is no more than a classroom lecture is cheating parishioners of what they need most—transformation.

Again Jeremiah, the greatest preacher in the Old Testament, provides a model. Jeremiah's message is empathetic. Webster defines empathy as "the projection of one's own personality into the personality of another in order to understand him better." Empathetic words travel "with feeling." Someone has defined empathy as "your problem becoming the ache in my heart." An empathetic word is not a disengaged, unattached, uncaring, "take it or leave it" word. The prophetical word knows nothing of neutrality. The word spoken by God's prophet is passionately affective and consequential for both speaker and hearer. There is intense resonance because the plight of the hearer is also the plight of the speaker. The prophetical working code presupposes that "your future is inextricably bound up with mine."

No prophet demonstrated more pathos than did Jeremiah. At times his grief was overwhelming and the pressure almost unbearable. "My sorrow is beyond healing. My heart is faint within me!" (8:18, NASB). The mental and physical stress was so intense that Jeremiah longed for cathartic release. "Oh that my head were waters and my eyes a fountain of tears that I might weep day and night for the slain of the daughter of my people!" (9:1, NASB). The bereaved hired professional mourners who would catalyze the collective catharsis during a time of death or calamity. "Thus says the LORD of hosts, 'Consider and call for the mourning women, that they may come, and send for the wailing women, that they may come! Let them make haste and take up a wailing for us, that our eyes may shed tears and our eyelids flow with water'" (vv. 17-18, NASB).

Jeremiah did not practice a detached professionalism. As he spoke, he wept. Unfortunately, such grotesque melancholy today would be assumed to be a neurosis of major proportions brought on by an infantile rage deeply imbedded in the unconscious. "Certainly Jeremiah must have had a hypercritical father and an overwhelming anal-retentive mother." It is difficult for us to understand that what really affected Jeremiah was not a deterministic event in his past but a foreboding future that he saw all too clearly.

Jeremiah proclaimed with passion. His words were emotively and imaginatively driven. They were objective in that he had insight into Judah's true condition. They were subjective in that he himself was Judean, an identity with his hearers that he could not escape. He could not escape this identification with his flock anymore than any responsible parent can say to his or her child, "Go ahead and try drugs and alcohol and see if I care." The proclamation of the gospel is enclosed with deep, passionate caring that cannot be shrugged off.

The cavalier manner in which contemporary preaching takes place is rendering the pulpit ineffective. The word has to be affective in order to be effective. Cool rational constructs will not change people. Urgent words that rain down like torrents are needed to wake drowsy parishioners anesthetized by trivial pursuits. The prophet speaks as if God means to be heard. God's message cloaked in a dry, pedantic discourse represents an incongruity. Prophetic communication is intensely hot. "'Is not My word like fire?' declares the LORD, 'and like a hammer which shatters a rock?'" (23:29, NASB).

The prophet/priestly message tells a story, which includes characters represented by people within the congregation. These people are not called out by name, but rather are composite profiles that depict the essential characteristics of both individual and collective humanity. These composite profiles will vary from culture to culture, which call for the pastor to be an astute observer of the fears, anxieties, guilt, and escapisms of a particular people. The congregation is the pastor's extended family whom he attempts to know intimately. The pastor is well aware of the skeletons in the closet and the family events that are embarrassing, if not outright shameful. This astute, open-eyed confession does not shrink from the truth: "Their nobles have sent their servants for water; they have come to the cisterns and found no water. They have returned with their vessels empty; they have been put to shame and humiliated, and they cover their heads" (14:3, NASB). Church should be the last place a person covers his or her head and hides from things as they really are. "Do not trust in deceptive words, saying, 'This is the temple of the LORD, the temple of the LORD, the temple of the LORD'" (7:4, NASB).

The sermon is the pastor telling his family story within the Christological drama. James Baldwin does this so effectively in *Go Tell It on the Mountain* that the anguish, despair, fear, and hope leap from the pages. Gabriel, the would-do-good preacher, in a moment of lust fathered a child. After banishing both mother and child who meet tragic ends, Gabriel lives a life of denial and guilt. Unattractive Deborah, his faithful wife, who was molested as a child, wants to believe the best of her husband, though she knows of his adulterous affair and bastard son. Gabriel's sister Florence, who experienced marriage and divorce from an alcoholic, thriftless husband, wants to believe in grace, but her faith is obscured by the prevailing hypocrisy not only of Gabriel but also of a church unable to effect lasting change for the good.

Elizabeth, who is now Gabriel's second wife, is forever haunted by the memory of her first love, Richard, who was falsely arrested by white men, savagely beaten, and who in his despair committed suicide. But during their courtship, she conceived a son who was born after Richard's death. The son, John, is rejected by Gabriel, who has placed all of his hopes and dreams in Roy, his true biological posterity. Roy is rebellious and violent, while John is pensive and searching. In spite of rejection by his father and the resultant psychological twistedness, John finds redemption in the darkness of a dysfunctional family. But John's plight represents more than his own family; he is a composite of the rejection of the black race, and the darkness of the Harlem Ghetto. Never was the longing for redemption so graphically depicted.

It was a sound of rage and weeping, which filled the grace, rage, and weeping from time set free, but bound now in eternity; rage that had no language, weeping with no voice—which yet spoke now, to John's startled soul, of boundless melancholy, of the bitterest patience, and the longest night; of the deepest water, the strongest chains, the most cruel lash; of humility most wretched, the dungeon most absolute, of love's bed defiled, and birth dishonored, and most bloody, unspeakable, sudden death. Yes, the darkness hummed with murder, the body in the water, the body in the fire, the body on the tree. John looked down the line of these armies of darkness, army upon army, and his soul whispered: **Who are these? Who are they?** And wondered: **Where shall I go?**[12]

Both Jeremiah's and Baldwin's passion were fueled by the perception of plight, the plight of their own people. The plight does not appear so desperate when camouflaged by the accumulation of "stuff" and the pursuit of middle-class aspirations. But the question needs to be asked, "Is the sting of sin any less for contemporary, middle-class Americans than it was for the seventh-century B.C. Judeans or for the 1940 Harlem Blacks?" One would think not, if he or she reads current headlines and listens to the heartbeats of those who sit in our pews. Any insightful and caring physician would become gravely concerned, perhaps even weep.

C. Relevant Speech

The word *relevant* is derived from the Latin *relevare*, "to lift up again." That which is relevant treads on familiar territory. Theology for most Americans is not familiar territory, unless it attaches itself to contemporary concerns, idioms, and landmarks. We visually encounter these landmarks on a daily basis: McDonald's, Nike, traffic jams, cell phones, sports, and TV. On the other hand, they present themselves more abstractly but even more forcefully as fear, stress, panic, depression, exhaustion, anxiety, and danger. Preaching that does not embrace life as it is daily lived falls on deaf ears. Life must be worked out in details and so must preaching. One of the secrets of theological imagination is turning the abstract into the concrete. Preaching is carried from the church to the home in shopping bags. The shoppers buy only those items that are relevant to their situation.

No book has ever been more realistic than the Bible. Its timelessness is preserved by its rawness. The book of beginnings is a treasure trove of predicaments that often seem hopelessly outside of God's sovereign grace. Adam, with salty sweat in his eyes and blisters on his hands, pines for the days of leisure back in the garden (with a lake full of bass). Noah's head throbs with a hangover as he remembers being at the helm of a ship.[13] A 100-year-old husband and a 90-year-old wife attend Lamaze classes, enduring the stares and gossip that penetrate their dignity. A 17-year-old boy looks at the rear end of a camel as his manacled feet walk across hot desert sand, a son of promise betrayed by jealous brothers. The stories that we find in Scripture are no less ideal than my story, your story, and the stories of those who hear us. Greed, lust, envy, treachery, deceit, avarice, malice, as well as forgiveness, love, and kindness are the stuff of life. The archetypical currents of life flow through good preaching. A failure to recognize these currents is a reductionism of the highest order.

David is now 70 years old. What do men think about when they are 70 years old? Security and significance. Late at night David sits in a smoke-filled hearth room, possibly staring at Goliath's sword in a trophy case just above the fireplace mantel. He calls for Joab, commander of the Israel army: "Go and conduct a census. There will be one question on the census questionnaire. 'Do you own a sword?'" Joab remonstrates, but the order of the king prevails. Nine months later the results of the census are tallied: 1.3 million men who can wield a sword.

The next morning the knock of the prophet Gad was more alarming than a 7.5 earthquake. The results of David's seemingly innocent act of independence was the death of 70,000 men. Let's see if I understand. God took only one life for David's sins of adultery and murder and the lives of 70,000 people for conducting a census. How could counting be so wrong? The essence of sin is lack of trust. It is a failure to do life's math God's way. One sword plus God equals God. Ten swords plus God equals God. One hundred swords plus God equals God. One thousand swords plus God equals God. The only part of the equation that really matters is God. The ruddy lad who slew Goliath without a sword became a slave of the sword. Accurate and precise preaching recognizes that Americans are some of the most enslaved people on earth. Nobody does more counting and calculating than we do. Preachers are especially guilty.

Some may think that in order to preach graphically, empathetically, and relevantly, one must possess either some innate talent or take infinitum preaching courses. Both may be helpful but not essential. Throughout history, effective preachers have employed plain language for plain people, using metaphors, symbols, and idioms that define everyday life. The incarnated Christ, who spoke of farms, treasures, banquets, and weddings is our prime example.

Ironically, the absence of technical training can be an asset for preaching. In speaking of the prophet, Heschel states that "the gift he is blessed with is not a skill, but rather the gift of being guided and restrained, of being moved and curbed."[14] Such was the recognition of the congregation in William Faulkner's *The Sound and the Fury*, regarding the preacher brought down from St. Louis to preach the Easter sermon. The first impression drew comparison to a small-aged monkey undersized in a shabby alpaca coat. The consternation and unbelief of the congregation was articulated in the whisper of a small boy to his mother, "En dey brung dat all de way fum Saint Looey."[15] The "dat" began slowly and methodically but gradually became like a worn small rock whelmed by the successive waves of his voice. With his body he seemed to feed the voice that, succubus like, had fleshed its teeth in him. And the congregation seemed to watch with its own eyes while the voice consumed him, until he was nothing and they were nothing and there was not even a voice, but instead their hearts were speaking toward one another in chanting measures beyond the need for words, so that when he came to rest against the reading desk, his monkey face lifted and his whole attitude, that of a serene tortured crucifix that transcended its shabbiness and insignificance and made it of no moment, a long moaning expulsion of breath rose from them, and a woman's single soprano: "Yes, Jesus!"[16]

For the oppressed and outcast race, the imagery was not lost. The "monkey" had trumpeted a blast of transcendent hope to those who had discovered through the experiences of life that only one hope really can be trusted. "Whut I see? Whut I see, O sinner? I sees resurrection in de light: sees de meek Jesus sayin Dey kilt me dat ye shall live again. I died dat dem what sees and believe shall never die."[17] On the way home, a mother weeping tears of joy, as she walked in the noonday sun, heard the words of her accompanying boy, "He sho a preacher man! He didn't look like much at first, but hush!? He seed de power in de glory. Yes, suh. He seed it, face to face, he seed it."[18]

Could it be that today's pastoral office is more concerned with "looks," appearance, than it is with substance? Samuel Chadwick reminded us who would be prophets that "indifference to religion is impossible where the preacher is a flame of fire . . . fire is self-evident. So is power!"[19] It is up to the pastor to see to it that there is abundant fuel. The world has the right to ministry ignited by a transcendent source. The fueling and the firing will have to be done on a daily basis. If not, it will be as disappointing as the leftovers from yesterday's breakfast. It is almost impossible to fool the guests. "God encounter" preachers must be "God encountered" preachers.

Notes

1. Paul Scott Wilson, *God Sense* (Nashville: Abingdon, 2001), 35.

2. Ibid., 55.

3. Ibid., 67.

4. Ibid., 68.

5. Abraham Heschel, *The Prophets* (New York: Harper and Row, 1962), 7.

6. Walter Fisher, *Human Communication as Narration: Toward a Philosophy of Reason, Value, and Action* (Columbia, S.C.: University of South Carolina Press, 1987), 63.

7. Mark Taylor and Esa Saarinen, *Imagologies* (New York: Routledge, 1994), 3.

8. Robert G. Lee, *Pay-Day, Someday* (Grand Rapids: Zondervan Publishing House, 1957), 9.

9. Ibid., 31.

10. Charles Bartow, *God's Human Speech* (Grand Rapids: William B. Eerdmans, 1997), 73.

11. Heschel, *The Prophets*, 26.

12. James Baldwin, *Go Tell It on the Mountain* (New York: Dell Publishing Company, 1953), 200-201.

13. Dennis Willis, "Noah Was a Good Man" in Eugene L. Lowery, *How to Preach a Parable* (Nashville: Abingdon Press, 1989), 42.

14. Heschel, *The Prophets*, 22.

15. William Faulkner, *The Sound and the Fury* (New York: Random House, 1984), 311.

16. Ibid., 367-68.

17. Ibid., 370.

18. Ibid., 371.

19. Samuel Chadwick, *The Way to Pentecost* (London: Hadden and Stoughton, 1972), 18.

For Further Reading

Baldwin, James. *Go Tell It on the Mountain*. New York: Dell Publishing Company, 1953.

Bartow, Charles. *God's Human Speech*. Grand Rapids: William B. Eerdmans, 1997.

Chadwick, Samuel. *The Way to Pentecost*. London: Hadden and Stoughton, 1972.

Faulkner, William. *The Sound and the Fury*. New York: Random House, 1984.

Heschel, Abraham. *The Prophets*. New York: Harper and Row, 1962.

Lee, Robert G. *Pay-Day, Someday*. Grand Rapids: Zondervan Publishing House, 1957.

Taylor, Mark, and Esa Saarinen. *Imagologies*. New York: Routledge, 1994.

Willis, Dennis. "Noah Was a Good Man" in Eugene L. Lowery, *How to Preach a Parable*. Nashville: Abingdon Press, 1989. See pages 42-78.

Wilson, Paul Scott. *God Sense*. Nashville: Abingdon, 2001.

James Earl Massey is dean emeritus and distinguished professor-at-large at Anderson University School of Theology in Anderson, Indiana. For 40 years, Dr. Massey has been an extraordinary preacher, teacher, and communicator of the gospel. He served as the senior pastor of the Metropolitan Church, Detroit, Michigan (1954-76); the campus minister of Anderson University, Anderson, Indiana (1969-77); a speaker on the *Christian Brotherhood Hour* radio broadcast (1977-82); dean of the Chapel of Tuskegee University, Tuskegee, Alabama (1984-90); and preacher-in-residence of Park Place Church of God, Anderson, Indiana (1994-95). He has preached and lectured at more than a hundred colleges, universities, and seminaries in the United States and on four continents. He is a life trustee of Asbury Theological Seminary and sits on the editorial boards of *Christianity Today, Leadership, Preaching,* and *The New Interpreter's Bible.* His published works include *The Responsible Pulpit* and *Designing the Sermon. Sharing Heaven's Music,* a collection of essays written by his colleagues in honor of Dr. Massey, is also available.

9

Proclaiming Holiness
The Divine Attribute and Christian Character
James Earl Massey

LARGE SECTIONS OF THE NEW TESTAMENT REPORT OR REFLECT how the first Christian preachers sought to help hearers learn about and appropriate the will and character of God, "the Holy One," in their personal experience. The concern of those preachers was to help believers live life on God's terms, indeed to link so fully with God that sharing in God's likeness—Christ being the observed measure—would be the result. A wide catena of texts deal with this concern. One such statement of intention came from Paul, whose goal in preaching and leading was "so that we may present everyone mature in Christ" (Col. 1:28, NRSV). Another is Peter's word in 2 Peter 1:4 about that same goal: "Thus he has given us, through these things, his precious and very great promises, so that through them you may escape from the corruption that is in the world because of lust, and may become participants of the divine nature" (NRSV). Texts like these draw attention to one of the most pertinent and positive claims made by the first Christian preachers: that God has ordained that those who surrender to His love will share in His likeness. Those preachers wanted all to know that becoming a Christian not only involves a change in one's experience but also a change in one's very being. They voiced this as the goal of the gospel. Many New Testament texts address this grand truth.

HOLINESS: THE DIVINE ATTRIBUTE

Every serious student of Scripture knows that the central concept among its vast teaching about God is God's holiness. God is to be understood as "the Holy One." This description about God's nature occurs with such frequency and emphasis, especially in the Old Testament, that it cannot be missed or overlooked.

As the Holy One, God is distinctly "Other." God is separated, marked off in nature from what is ordinary, common, or human. God is so distinctive and unique, so absolute in perfection and purity, so utterly peculiarly Other in being that to realize His presence is to experience a radical awe. Both Testaments supply us with multiplied instances when some human recoiled when confronted by the divine Presence.

But God is holy Person, which means that His "Otherness" does more than occasion a radical awe. This "Otherness" also occasions a radical attractiveness that invites communion. The God about whom both the Testaments witness, the God and Father of Jesus the Christ, is uniquely separate but is not remote nor utterly removed. His presence provokes awe, yet He always seeks to relate, eagerly appealing to share himself and His very life and holiness with humans.

Since this is true, it is important to understand in what way, and to what extent, God grants believers to share His holiness. This is a question that theological camps have debated, some claiming more than God makes available to humanity and others claiming less than God intended to bestow. Does God only impute His holiness to us, or does God actually impart His holiness to believers? Based upon multiple New Testament texts that encourage believers to seek the very character of God, the Wesleyan tradition has long maintained that every believer can lay claim upon God's holiness in more than a figurative manner because holiness of life is far more than a figure of speech.

We who preach can proclaim that God has shown us His holiness on our human level in Jesus Christ, His Son. The Sonship of Jesus is real, and it is revelational. The character of His life as depicted in the Gospels is a manifestation of holiness in the flesh. The writer to the Hebrews reported that Jesus the Son of God "is the reflection of God's glory and the exact imprint of God's very being" (1:3, NRSV). Jesus himself made the claim that "whoever sees me sees him who sent me" (John 12:45, NRSV), and "whoever has seen me has seen the Father" (14:9, NRSV). God has clearly revealed His holiness on our level in the unique Sonship of Jesus. God is Jesus' Father in both mode and manner, which we are not able completely to understand or explain. The New Testament witnesses to the earthly life of Jesus and did not get sidetracked over metaphysical questions about His genesis or descent as divine Son; they rightly and wisely celebrated Jesus as Savior, giving due honor to God the Father who sent Him. John 1:18 says, "No one has ever seen God. It is God the only Son, who is close to the Father's heart, who has made him known" (NRSV).

Jesus as revealing Son is a necessary truth for us to keep in focus because what we are to preach about sharing in the holiness of God is related to what is exemplified in Jesus. As believers on His name, we stand related to Jesus as the one who "gave [us] power to become children of God" (John 1:12, NRSV). Our adoption into God's family is derived through Jesus' relation to God. Thus we note Paul's praiseful word about this: "Blessed be the God and Father of our Lord Jesus Christ, who has blessed us in Christ with every spiritual blessing in the heavenly places, just as he chose us in Christ before the foundation of the world to be holy and blameless before him in love. He destined us for adoption as his children through Jesus Christ, according to the good pleasure of his will, to the praise of his glorious grace that he freely bestowed on us in the Beloved" (Eph. 1:3-6, NRSV). Behind it all stands the holy God, working His will through Jesus Christ in our interest and to His honor. Jesus is not only God's model Son but also our means and model for a derived holy likeness to God the Father.

CHRISTIAN HOLINESS THROUGH LIFE IN CHRIST

Our preaching should invite hearers to Christian holiness—that quality of life and those distinctive character traits made possible through openness to the indwelling Spirit of Christ. This holiness is not the product of some regional, national, or denominational influence, nor is it conformity to some pattern of conduct peculiar to some defensive group rationale. Christian holiness involves being clothed "with the new self, created according to the likeness of God" (Eph. 4:24, NRSV). Christian holiness is a derived result. It is definite and distinctive.

1. Our derived share in God's holiness is, first of all, _individual,_ because each believer can experience God personally. The whole self is called into the transaction with God that conversion initiates.

Our human nature, marred by sin, can originally reflect only our natural heritage of flesh, but by spiritual rebirth—by being "born from above" (John 3:7, NRSV) through conversion, we can meaningfully intersect with God's will for us and live on new terms as adopted members of God's family. But this stage is anticipatory; it is intended to usher us into a fuller share in family life with God, especially experiencing in ourselves the character of our Father and bringing honor to God through dedicated living and focused service. Preaching on Christian holiness places before the hearers the possibility, necessity, excellence, and availability of this fuller and richer experience.

2. Our derived share in God's holiness is also _identifiable._ God by His Spirit shapes new character traits. Meister Eckhart (c. 1260—1327)

identified Christian character as "a habitual will," by which he meant the will transformed into instinct, complete self-unity, a oneness of the self and self-interest with the will of God. Life then is adjusted to God's scales. The Holy Spirit works within us with potency and immediacy as we remain surrendered to God's claim on us.

Christian character is best described as Christlikeness. The identifiable traits are set forth among the listed "fruit of the Spirit" (Gal. 5:22-23). This "fruit," these Christlike traits of character, is produced as the Holy Spirit of God does His critical and creative work within us. He brings the many elements of personality into focus and draws tight the previously loose strings of personal life, holding them with the sure grip of God. Irenaeus (c. 175-c.195), who faithfully followed the apostolic tradition, was referring to the Holy Spirit's inward ministry when he commented that the Holy Spirit "adjusts us to God."[1] Other relations and influences in life tend to diminish the self or diffuse and dissipate the life. But the Holy Spirit works within us to shape us in conformity to a new pattern, a holy model, as we "cleanse ourselves from every defilement of body and spirit, making holiness perfect in the fear of God" (2 Cor. 7:1, NRSV). The result of this is readily identifiable.

3. Our derived share in God's holiness is *intelligible*. This kind of experience, this set of results, can be expressed in the form of definite doctrines and a set of convictions. Such noble features and healthy aspects of life make sense. We can call attention to what has happened and is happening, and we can interpret to others what it means to us and for us. It has always been sensible to live by a pattern and follow a path that honors God.

4. Our derived share in God's holiness is also *instrumental*. This sharing readies us for a destiny in God's will and it enables us to fulfill the works of the law, with "love [as] the fulfilling of the law" (Rom. 13:10, NRSV). That love is a divine issue "because God's love has been poured into our hearts through the Holy Spirit that has been given to us" (5:5, NRSV).

Sharing in holiness deepens the believer's commitment to what is vital, what is sacred, what is necessary. The holy life is dedicated to a high and honorable standard of living, worthy values, and a sustained commitment to regard these distinctives to the honor of God. But sharing in holiness also orients us for caring. Just as there are sacred distinctives, there are social duties that are best handled through strategic services from a caring heart. John Wesley (1703-91) wrote: "The Gospel of Christ knows of no religion but social; no holiness, but social holiness.

Faith working by love is the length and breadth and depth and height of Christian perfection."[2]

SOME PRINCIPLES FOR PREACHING ABOUT HOLINESS

Since holiness is not only a divine attribute but also a level of life, it is a vital subject for study and preaching. The earnest preacher will live daily with the Scriptures, striving to ascertain a full impact from their central message, in order to understand, live by, and wisely use scriptural themes and emphases. Holiness is one of these themes.

1. *Study the pulpit work of leading holiness exponents.* In addition to being aids to acquaint us with apt preaching styles, some of the holiness exponents can acquaint us with model ways to handle holiness texts. As I have given attention to preaching this great theme, I have profited from reading the works of A(iden) W(ilson) Tozer (1897—1963), whose weighted words were carefully chosen to convey the biblical vision of holiness with clarity, conciseness, and appeal. His *Pursuit of God* (1948) and *Knowledge of the Holy* (1961) are Christian classics whose biblical base, spiritual depth, and aesthetic appeal are inspirational and highly instructive. The same can be said about the published pulpit work of the soundly biblical and highly articulate Paul Stromberg Rees (1900-1991). His *Christian: Commit Yourself* (1957) and *Church in God* (an expository series on Thessalonians) provide due guidance in handling the holiness emphasis in preaching. The pulpit work of William M. Greathouse must also be mentioned. This holiness advocate's trenchant for drawing meaning directly from the biblical text and for following the movement of the text in shaping the sermon made his pulpit work exegetically apt and homiletically appealing. In his book *Wholeness in Christ: Toward a Biblical Theology of Holiness* (1998), Greathouse has offered a thoroughly documented statement about biblical holiness after a lifetime of exploring the subject and reading contemporary literature.

In the late 20th century Beacon Hill Press of Kansas City published six volumes in a series titled *Great Holiness Classics*. The publisher conceived and launched the project "to provide a representative compilation of the best holiness literature in a format readily accessible to the average minister, thus providing: (1) the preservation of the essential elements of our holiness heritage; (2) an overview of the broad scope of the holiness message; (3) a norm for holiness theology, proclamation, and practice; (4) a succinct reference work on holiness; and (5) a revival of the best of the out-of-print holiness classics."[3] Volume 5 in the series was a collection of sermons on holiness, sermons representing the time span from John Wesley (1703-91) to the latter part of the 20th century. Forty-four sermons were included: some dealt with understanding the doctrine and emphases of holiness, some with how the experience of holiness (sanctification) is sought and gained, some with the Holy Spirit's ministry in helping believers live the holy life, some with the social implications of holy living, and some with proclaiming holiness. All considered, the preachers and sermons featured in the volume were fairly representative of their generations, most were from historic orthodox communions, and nearly all offered a handling of the holiness theme that was insightfully doctrinal and practical without being doctrinaire. Throughout the volume the preachers handled the subject of holiness with clarity and tolerance. The intent of the volume was to focus light on the subject, offer angles and emphases for treating the subject of holiness, and provide documented specimens for reading and study from acknowledged advocates of Christian holiness. *Holiness Preachers and Preaching* was only one of a number of such volumes produced by publishers intent to honor the biblical teaching of holiness, but I have highlighted this book because holiness advocates from many denominations contributed to it and because it is a resourceful compendium conveying how holiness texts have been understood and proclaimed through preaching across several centuries.

2. *In planning to preach on holiness, be mindful of the functional forcefulness of the holiness-text you choose, and let it influence your handling of the text.*

By the "functional forcefulness of a text" I refer to how that text is worded and the way the biblical writer used those words. Often because of our familiarity with some portion of Scripture, we tend to miss or overlook the dynamism in the religious language the biblical writers used. When one takes time to explore and classify their sentence forms and the functions they intended the forms to achieve, the meaning and significance of their writings become all the more evident and even eventful for us.

Early in the 1970s, in the course of my career-long work of teaching seminarians and pastors to preach as servants of biblical truths, letting Scripture substance influence even the shape of the sermon, I began a fresh study of the New Testament. Influenced by semantics and studies that deal with religious language as a specialized category, I took a prolonged look into the functions the New Testament writers intended by their dynamic use of language. Beginning with the Epistles, I carefully examined the sentence units within them. I isolated and interrogated the many sentence forms and functions, intent to discern and capture more fully what was said and what was meant. I was satisfied with nothing less than the actual "meaning" and "significance" of the texts. In time, I prepared and presented a paper to the Wesleyan Theological Society in which I categorized the treatment of Christian holiness in the Epistles using three major function-headings: "statements" about holiness, "expressions" regarding holiness, and "prescriptives" to live holy lives.[4] Further details about these function-headings are in order because they can help the preacher who is intent on treating the holiness theme with integrity, incisiveness, and insight.

Semanticists have pointed out that in uttering a sentence in our everyday use of words we do one or more of four things: (1) we make a *statement*, that is, we assert or affirm some fact; (2) we make an *expression*, an utterance in which emotion and impulse show themselves; (3) we voice a *prescriptive*, that is, we say something to direct someone about what is to be done; (4) we sometimes utter what semanticists refer to as a *performative*, which describes our use of words to say something that creates a new state of affairs, like making a promise.[5]

The first three of these categories—statements, expressions, and prescriptives—are especially helpful in ascertaining the function level of the many holiness texts found in the New Testament. By "holiness texts" I refer to sentence units that utilize one or more of the words based on the Greek root **hag** and occur in a context directly related to the concern for Christian holiness as exemplified in behavior, codes, attitude, and so forth. The categories "statements" and "prescriptives" are the most plentiful of sentence functions among the many holiness texts. This is understandable because the sentences are in epistles addressed to believers to guide and sustain them in righteousness and obedience of faith. The writers of the Epistles used numbers of prescriptives, telling us what is to be done. As we study the statements (indicatives) and the prescriptives (imperatives) we see how these two categories relate to Christian experience.

Since the New Testament treatment of Christian holiness involves statements, expressions, and prescriptives, we gain a clear view of human life as God wills it. The New Testament expressions about holiness make clear assertions and a claim meant to gain attention and challenge us to action. The New Testament expressions about holiness convey excitement about a quality of life that is real, valuable, engaging, and progressive. The New Testament prescriptives about holiness are unsparing in what they stress for us and demand from us; the imperatives voiced in prescriptive texts are used with high warrant, strict realism, and decisive intent. The preacher who examines the many holiness texts from these angles cannot fail to understand that they witness about a higher level of life that God has opened to us. He or she sees that preaching about holiness is necessary to inform believers about it. God's concern is our practical holiness, the enhancement of our lives, our fulfillment of His ethical and moral demands, and our readiness for service in the world as bearers of His Spirit and character.

3. *In preaching about holiness, let the text dictate the approach to be used.* Texts that hold a "statement" about holiness suggest a doctrinal approach in the sermon, while texts that offer an "expression" about holiness can be used illustratively in treating the experience. Holiness texts that are prescriptives usually dictate, by their very nature, that the sermon be shaped to voice an unmistakable call to the hearer to enter fully into the holy life.

I have explained a holiness text as a text that utilizes one or more holiness terms in its sentence function and deals with some ethical or behavioral claim God makes upon the believer. Richard S. Taylor, a noted holiness scholar, offers a more expansive view of a holiness text. In his book *Preaching Holiness Today*, Taylor wrote: "A holiness text is any passage which, within itself, in its contextual relations and in its inner meaning, is related to the will of God that men should be holy."[6] Taylor also identified three levels of such texts: (1) those texts in which the holiness thrust is unmistakable, texts that are plainly oriented toward doctrinal statement and analysis; (2) texts in which the holiness emphasis is implicit rather than explicit; and (3) texts that are more or less illustrative of the holiness experience—either as picture or illustration and application of the truth about the experience. Taylor advised that when preaching to teach about or to interpret holiness, unmistakably explicit holiness texts should be used, that texts that treat holiness implicitly rather than explicitly should be used inferentially, and that texts that only illustrate holiness should only be used illustratively. The principle advised here is that the method one uses in preaching Christian holiness should relate to the kind of text used.

Notes

1. Quoted by F. W. Dillistone, *The Holy Spirit in the Life of Today* (London: Canterbury Press, 1946), 10.

2. *The Works of the Rev. John Wesley*, A.M. (London: John Mason, 1856), Vol. XIV, 305.

3. See A. F. Harper, "Understanding the Great Holiness Classics," in Vol. 5, *Holiness Preachers and Preaching,* ed. W. E. McCumber (Kansas City: Beacon Hill Press of Kansas City, 1989), 11-12.

4. See James Earl Massey, "Semantics and Holiness: A Study in Holiness-Texts Functions," *Wesleyan Theological Journal* 10 (Spring 1975): 60-69.

5. On these categorical desciptions, see Anders Jeffner, *The Study of Religious Language* (London: SCM Press Ltd., 1972), esp. 11-12, 68-104. See also J. L. Austin, *How to Do Things with Words,* ed. J. O. Urmson (New York: Oxford University Press, Galaxy Book, 1965); John Wilson, *Language and the Pursuit of Truth* (Cambridge: University Press, 1960), esp. 47-74.

6. Richard S. Taylor, *Preaching Holiness Today* (Kansas City: Beacon Hill Press of Kansas City, 1968). See esp. chap. 7 on "Principles of Interpretation," 90-108.

For Further Reading

Abbey, Merrill R. *Living Doctrine in a Vital Pulpit.* Nashville: Abingdon Press, 1964.

Cox, James W. *A Guide to Biblical Preaching.* Nashville: Abingdon Press, 1976.

Greathouse, William M. *Wholeness in Christ: Toward a Biblical Theology of Holiness.* Kansas City: Beacon Hill Press of Kansas City, 1998.

Massey, James Earl. *The Sermon in Perspective: A Study of Communication and Charisma.* Grand Rapids: Baker Book House, 1976.

———. *Designing the Sermon: Order and Movement in Preaching.* Nashville: Abingdon Press, 1980.

McCumber, William E., ed. *Holiness Preachers and Preaching* in Great Holiness Classics, Vol. 5. Kansas City: Beacon Hill Press of Kansas City, 1989.

McGraw, James, comp. *The Holiness Pulpit.* Kansas City: Beacon Hill Press, 1957.

———. *The Holiness Pulpit,* No. 2. Kansas City: Beacon Hill Press of Kansas City, 1974.

Turner, George Allen. *The Vision Which Transforms.* Kansas City: Beacon Hill Press, 1964.

Marva J. Dawn is a prolific writer and popular Christian speaker. A theologian and church musician, she holds, in addition to four master's degrees, a Ph.D. in Christian Ethics and the Scriptures from the University of Notre Dame. She is an educator with Christians Equipped for Ministry of Vancouver, Washington, and Teaching Fellow in Spiritual Theology at Regent College in Vancouver, British Columbia. She has worked with pastors and seminaries throughout North America and in Australia, China, England, Hong Kong, Japan, Madagascar, New Zealand, Norway, Poland, Scotland, and Singapore. Marva's recent titles include *Unfettered Hope: A Call to Faithful Living in an Affluent Society; Joy in Our Weakness: A Gift of Hope from the Book of Revelation; Powers, Weakness, and the Tabernacling of God; The Unnecessary Pastor: Rediscovering the Call* (cowritten with Eugene Peterson); and *A Royal Waste of Time* (which includes samples of her sermons). Marva is Joy-fully married to Myron Sandberg.

10
Preaching the Whole Character of God

Marva J. Dawn

❧ DIALECTICAL TENSIONS INCESSANTLY COMPLICATE OUR LIVES. CHIL-DREN need mentoring parents, yet they must learn to fly on their own. Immigrants struggle to adapt to their new country while they still cherish the customs, language, and identity of their homeland. Church leaders experience the challenge to be forthright about their visions and compelling in their influence, without falling into either a false pride or a false humility.

Preachers constantly balance dialectical tensions—in our personal lives, in the preaching task, and in the subject matter about which we preach. The preaching task is extremely hard in this era of visual wizardry and glitzy spectacle, when "words" are not trusted.[1] At the same time, preaching can be a pivotal gift for a confused and troubled world. How do we hold these tensions together and persist in the role?

We can hold the tensions of our lives and preaching in better balance if we more thoroughly know and proclaim God's whole character with all its dialectical interplay. The more thoroughly we wrestle with supposed contradictions in order not to slight any dimensions of God's character, the more we are equipped to set before the people for whom we preach the different facets of God—and, consequently, the more all of us will learn the language of faith for all the circumstances of our lives.

THE LANGUAGE OF FAITH

I speak of faith as a language to avoid two extremes detrimental to Christianity.[2] One is to reduce faith merely to intellectual agreement with doctrinal propositions—a definition most often held by more conservative groups that tend to make faith rigid, narrow, ostracizing, and without enfleshment. Doctrinal truths are indeed essential, but they are only the bones, the skeleton of the Body of Christ. They need to be not only thought but also lived. On the other hand, faith can't be reduced simply to expressions of common religious feelings or impulses. This understanding is usually held by more liberal groups, especially those who insist that there is no difference between Christianity and other faiths, such as Islam or Buddhism.

Christian faith, however, abides in the historical particularity of Jesus of Nazareth. Truths of His preexistence in the Triune Godhead, His incarnation, life of teaching and suffering, death on a cross, resurrection, and ascension are the essential grammar of the Christian language and the means through which we learn more clearly all other speech about God. These doctrinal bones, furthermore, are enfleshed in the Church,[3] for believers who follow Jesus take up their cross, too, and daily die to themselves so that they might be raised by the Father into the new life with the Son through the power of the Holy Spirit.

True faith is a lived language, constantly developing its vocabulary by new encounters with other dimensions of the whole character of the Triune God. We learn any language by hearing, speaking, reading, writing it, and most importantly, by being immersed in the culture of those who speak and live it. This is why worship and community life are so essential.

In the midst of the whole milieu of the lived speech of the Church, preachers model both the speech and the life. In fact, preachers "stand before" (a literal translation of the Greek participle *proistamenous* in 1 Thess. 5:12) and thereby offer listeners new speech learned in their study by which the church glimpses new visions of God's kingdom. The people inhabit those visions so that they might be ambassadors of that kingdom wherever they are during the week.

OUR DATA-BIT, NONDIALECTICAL WORLD

Christianity's language is especially hard to preach in the 21st century. Many people reject Christian faith because they can't hold in tension some of the dialectical pairs we will explore below. Christians themselves have difficulty balancing these truths and living the faith well in authentically following Jesus.

For example, how should Christians respond to the continuing and ever-escalating violence between Israel and Palestine? We struggle for a vocabulary that can both indict those who inflict harm and yet have compassion for all those in the world whose hunger and homelessness drive them to suicide missions. How do we bring oppressors to righteous justice and simultaneously develop genuine justice for the oppressed?

Our inability to think dialectically is aggravated by society's de-pendence on computers, which operate by means of data bits that are either on or off. Similarly, political rhetoric (other nations are either good or evil) heightens an _either/or_ mentality. To think _both/and_ requires much more effort and careful nuancing.

Consequently, many people disregard the importance of thinking things through clearly, especially in connection with God. For example, _if_ God is sovereignly powerful (as Christianity confesses), then why does God allow continued tragedies of terrorists' destructive work, of hunger and homelessness, of personal and global suffering? Such things don't make sense, so it seems easier, less traumatic, to give up on God altogether.

Perhaps the hardest texts to preach these days are those that speak of God's wrath. We'd rather have a cozy God who helps us feel better. Why does the _good news_ often seem like such bad news? Without pon-dering dialectically the Triune God's whole character, many find it im-possible to believe and so turn to other, less confusing gods.

"DON'T LET THOSE ELBOWS FALL TO THE SIDE!"

Let me offer an image for dialectical thinking to help us ponder God's whole character and preach it in ways that don't get bogged down in abstractions. Curl in all your fingers at their second knuckle and in-terlock the finger sets of your two hands. Then raise your elbows until your forearms are parallel to the floor and your elbows point out right and left. Now pull each elbow further out, but keep your fingers inter-locked so that your arms can't split apart. Do you feel a strain on your upper arm muscles? Keep pulling!

The elbows represent two seemingly contradictory truths. Both truths can be maintained in a dialectical balance only if you pull both arms equally and your hands remain clasped in the center. If your fingers don't remain gripped or if your arms don't pull equally, the truths the el-bows represent will tilt to one side or the other or the combination of the two will fall apart. If you keep pulling hard and maintain a firm grasp, the dialectic truths the elbows represent are held in balance. It takes good strong muscles to keep the dialectical arms together, just as it takes vigorous theological muscle to keep spiritual truths balanced.

Much of Christian history is characterized by imbalances between sets of truths in which seemingly opposite sides are over- or under-ac-centuated. For example, major heresies arose when beliefs that Jesus is both true God and true man were not kept together. Various forms of those same heresies—denying His true enfleshment or, more often, His divinity—have reappeared in our time. Preachers need strong theological muscles to help listeners keep both sides in their understanding of Jesus.

Such doctrinal developments in Christian history are critically important. If we don't know Jesus truly as both God and man, we cannot really understand what His salvation entails. Without faithfulness to all that the Scriptures tell us about who Jesus was and is and will be, we cannot persist in the fullness of His way of life.

DIALECTICS IN JESUS

We start with Jesus to know the whole character of God, for we believe the Messiah reveals most fully who God is. As the early Christians wrestled with the significance of the events they had witnessed, they realized that God must be Triune, since Jesus himself is divine and brings us into His own intimacy with His Father through the gift of their Spirit.

But Jesus himself is no "easy read." We'll never get done preaching the dialectical truths of Jesus if we want the Church's faith ever to grow toward maturity.

The paradoxes begin at His conception—that the Lord of the cosmos should so humble himself to be born into poverty and oppression from a teenaged peasant virgin. Surely if we preach this dialectic more fully, we won't have such romanticized Christmases that fail to equip Christians to follow Jesus into present incarnations of the Gospel in the midst of the same sorts of poverty and oppression.

To preach this dialectic fully, for example, would cause us to admit and repent that we (most North American Christians) are the rich who are sent away empty in Mary's Magnificat (Luke 1:53). Simultaneously, we rejoice hopefully because this Child has come for just such hopeless sinners as we; indeed, "His mercy is for those who fear him" (v. 50, NRSV).

We need both elbows in this dialectic. To preach only the emptiness of our riches leads to despair. To proclaim only God's mercy makes us think we deserve it.

LAW AND GOSPEL

Martin Luther summarized this crucial dialectic that we don't deserve God's mercy and yet that Christ came to give it to us with the terms *Law* and *Gospel*. This word *Law* doesn't mean specific laws or rules, but the whole truth of alienation from God through our rebellions, misconceptions, omissions, and misdeeds. In short, we are under the Law because our essential nature is to be sinners, inclined to make ourselves our own gods. The Gospel is the *good news* that God in Christ reconciled sinners to Himself—not only forgiving their specific sins but also re-creating them anew by the Holy Spirit's power to be saints in the fullness of Triune grace.

Luther's insight is crucial for preaching, though with modifications for our times. Richard Lischer urges us not to hammer our listeners with the Law, but to engage them in "an experiential process of discovery . . . whose end is self-recognition, repentance, new vision, and participation in the life of the community."[4]

The truth of Christ's atonement is not good news unless we know we need it. We preach the Law (in Lischer's process) in order to bring listeners into the presence of the God who holds us accountable. We proclaim the Gospel so that they encounter the God who loves to rescue, reconcile, re-create, and renew us.

These elbows of Law and Gospel must be held in a careful tension. To bombard people with the Law makes them stiffen with resistance or plunge into despair. Positively, to enable people to understand more deeply all the elements of the Law of sin and death is to give them tools for making sense of the evils, pain, brokenness, and sinfulness they discover in themselves and receive from others in the fallenness of the world, to stir them to repentance, and to prepare the way for the coming of the Savior.

To fall off the elbow of the Gospel is to plummet into antinomianism, to say, "I like to sin and God likes to forgive; isn't that a nice arrangement?"—or to cascade into the hubris of thinking we could be worthy of God's grace. One error cheapens Christ's atonement and the other ignores it.

To preach the Gospel in a nuanced combination with the Law equips listeners with a sense of how rich God's love is that Christ bore the cost of grace and how full that grace is that it frees us *from* the Law's oppression and *for* glad obedience to God's laws.

HOLINESS AND LOVE

The Law/Gospel dialectic exists because God is both holiness and love. Holiness cannot tolerate our sinfulness; love makes a way for it to be forgiven. God's holiness prevents love from being mere sentimentality; His love prevents holiness from being impersonal. Both must be maintained, and neither must be allowed to dominate for encountering God truly.

To accentuate only God's holiness destroys freedom to "be holy" ourselves through grace. Only by love are we re-created, indwelt, and transformed into both justified sainthood and sanctified living like the saints we are by Christ's work.

Preaching only love eliminates absolutes by which to name our world's evils. Holiness empowers us to be righteously angry about sin, never flagging in our zeal to counteract injustice (in spite of nonsuccess in the world's terms), and emboldened to stand firmly against the principalities and powers.

We dare not divide holiness and love among the persons of the Trinity as have those who view the Father as a patriarchal holy oppressor demanding the sacrifice of His own loving Son. Instead the Scriptures clearly state that *"in Christ God* was reconciling the world to himself" (2 Cor. 5:19, NRSV, emphasis added). We dare not remove love from the Holy Father who **so** loved the world that in His own self-donation He gave us His Son.

Similarly, we dare not take holiness from the Son. Some time ago I heard a preacher reduce the gospel to "Jesus loves you and accepts you just as you are" without any sense that we don't deserve it or that His holiness is too loving and too holy to let us stay that way.[5]

Christ's inextricable union of holiness and love is clearly manifested in the dialectical oddity that though divine, He thoroughly submits in perfectly loving obedience to His Father's will. Truly this is a crucial mystery to keep before ourselves and our listeners when we preach.

Christ's holy and loving obedience involves another dialectical pair central for faith and demonstrated graphically in the events of Luke 9. Jesus' transfiguration in 9:28-36 is preceded both by Peter recognizing Jesus as God's Christ (v. 20) and Jesus foretelling His suffering and death and calling the disciples to deny themselves, take up their cross, and follow Him in the same sort of suffering (vv. 21-26).

Christ's transcendence would not benefit us at all without His atoning work as our substitute. Only because in His immanence He came down to be the True Light *in* the world (John 1:9-11) could He give us power to become the children of God (v. 12).

Dialectically, without the vision of Christ's transfiguration we don't have hope that enables us to follow Jesus in bearing crosses. And did the transfiguration event also give Jesus hope to endure His own suffering? As "the pioneer and perfecter of our faith" Jesus for the Joy set before Him "endured the cross, disregarding its shame" (Heb. 12:2, NRSV). He demonstrated His human need for companionship by asking the disciples to watch *with Him* in Gethsemane. Might the glorified Moses and

Elijah, who spoke with Jesus "of his departure, which he was about to accomplish at Jerusalem" (Luke 9:31, NRSV), have reminded Him of this eschatological Joy? These mysteries are raised by the dialectical combinations of suffering and glory, immanence and transcendence, humanity and divinity.

The church year equips us with a more complete picture of all that Christ is and has done for us. Does our preaching display over time this dialectical fullness to undergird our listeners' understanding of their own salvation?

THE HOLY SPIRIT'S HOLINESS AND LOVE

Have you thought much about the Holy Spirit's character? We can see the Father's attributes in Jesus, but the Spirit is usually perceived quite amorphously. However, if God is truly Trinity—and not separated persons functioning in divided modes, as the heresies distort—then the divine persons coequally, coinherently share both holiness and love. Yet the Scriptures tell us little about the Spirit except the results of His indwelling. We know the Spirit through His work in our lives.

Does not the Spirit's holiness draw us into repentance and sorrow? Doesn't the Spirit's love propel us into faith and fill us with wonder at the Trinity's immense grace, which the Spirit communicates? Thus, these dialectical attributes in the Holy Spirit both cause us to perceive them more clearly in the Father and the Son and also compel us to respond in kind.

FEAR AND LOVE

Martin Luther wisely knew that human responses to the dialectics of holiness and love, Law and Gospel, must also be dialectical—a combination of fear and love, with *fear* meaning neither terror nor simple reverence and respect. Rather, the biblical "fear of the LORD" that is "the beginning of wisdom" is profound cognizance that multiple forces make it impossible for us to please God in our own strength: evil powers harm, societal temptations beckon, and we ourselves wrestle with a fallen nature that wants to be its own god. Luther summarizes these as "the devil, the world, and our flesh." A healthy fear of these forces makes us vigilant, intentional, dependent upon grace, and grateful for God's deliverance. A healthy fear of God makes us repentant, humble, and Joyfull because we are delivered by grace. John Newton epitomized this in the lines, "'Twas grace that taught my heart to fear, / and grace those fears relieved."

Our love for God is deeper when strongly counterbalanced by biblical fear—for then God's love is always a bright treasure, a glorious gift, a thorough liberation. We can never take grace for granted if we fearfully know the depths of our fallenness. Thus, our response is a profound gratefulness that amplifies our love—and, consequently, our obedience.

Luther's catechism to instruct believers in the faith explores all Ten Commandments in terms of fear and love; this dialectical response to God's fullness frees us for more comprehensive obedience. He instructs, for example, concerning the commandment not to kill, "We should fear and love God that we may not hurt nor harm our neighbor in his body, but help and befriend him in every bodily need"[6] and, regarding the commandment not to steal, "We are to fear and love God so that we do not take our neighbor's money or property, or get them in any dishonest way, but help him to improve and protect his property and means of making a living."[7]

Preaching comparably can suggest multifold responses for loving our world—generosity, hospitality, reconciliation, peacemaking, justice building—but these are evoked more strongly if the dialectical character of the God who elicits them is proclaimed more fully.

GOD'S WRATH

How, then, do we preach biblical texts about God's wrath? Many preachers avoid them entirely, for it's not a word people want to hear these days—or ever! But we lose impetus for fighting injustice if we ignore God's wrath, even as we buttress a case for more evil in the world if we teach God's wrath wrongly. Osama bin Laden claimed to be rightly exercising God's wrath in his strategies for 9-11-01.

How we place wrath in the dialectics of God's whole character has enormous implications for our preaching in the new world spewed out by that day's explosions. Some preachers since then have implied that the U.S. is good (like God?) and thus is able to vent God's wrath against evil nations. But that immensely mistaken perspective puts God's wrath entirely under the holiness side of its dialectical tension with love.

Old Testament professor Terence Fretheim clarifies that God regularly gives motivations for His anger and thereby shows that wrath is not a divine attribute (which would entail an eternal dualism of wrath and love). Rather, God's anger (in contrast to humans', which is infected with sin) is always exercised in the service of life, is always relational, and is connected, especially by the prophets, with divine grief. Thus, wrath is a sign of His love.

The biblical texts cite human wickedness as the motivation for God's wrath in about half of the settings. Three-fourths are marked by infidelity to God. *Never* is wrath vented to protect God or because the LORD's moral sense is offended. [Thus, wrath is not so much a function of God's holiness.] Instead, God's wrath is part of His saving purposes. One of its goals is to end indifference to oppression and thereby make a future possible to those who have no hope.[8]

Our preaching on texts regarding God's wrath is profoundly changed if we view God's anger as coming from the loving side of the dialectic of holiness and love—or at least from the intersection between the two. We also increase our ability to respond properly to evils in other people and in the world if we vent our anger out of love for everyone involved!

ONE AND THREE

At several points our consideration of the dialectics we preach has brought us face-to-face with the dialectic of the Trinity's oneness and threeness. This is indeed the greatest mystery of all. How could God be one God and yet three persons? How could He be three persons yet only one God?

Our mistake, of course, is to try to understand it when all we can do is proclaim it. However, examining the doctrine's historical development enables us at least a bit to see how the Church got "Trinity" from the events of Jesus of Nazareth.[9]

Theologizing began early when Jesus, whom the apostles knew truly as a man, was also revealed to them (in stages as John 1—2 illustrates) as Messiah, coequal with God. Over the course of history and against contradictory heresies the Church formulated the relation of Father, Son, and Spirit as distinct, but not divided. Strongly monotheistic out of Christianity's Jewish roots and in opposition to the Greek and Roman pantheons, early Christians at Nicaea insisted that God had one being (*ousia*) but three substances (*hypostatis*). A huge problem arose when Western Christians used the Latin *persona* for God's threeness, which implies three distinct personalities and so splits the Trinity too far apart. The Orthodox doctrine of *perichoresis*, the intertwining dance of the Trinity, seems to keep the three and one in better balance.

This dialectical tension has enormous practical consequences—so we keep proclaiming it. Letting it slip apart leads to such confusions as making Jesus only human still or forgetting the Father's immanence and thinking Him far away in His eternal being.

Some contemporary vocabulary shifts are ultimately destructive to Trinitarian doctrinal truths. For example, some preachers today refuse to call God "Father" (largely in reaction to falsely patriarchal uses of the term, though the name applied to God implies not gender but intimacy). However, to call God "Mother" instead is to forget the two natures of Christ. Jesus was a true man whose mother was Mary (the *theotokos* or "God-bearer"). We call God "Father" because Jesus urges us to do so and is the High Priest who ushers us into His own intimacy with His Abba.[10]

Some preachers avoid calling God "Father" by substituting "Creator, Redeemer, Sanctifier" for the Trinity's names. However, this supplants names with functions and fails to comprehend how all the persons of the Trinity create and redeem and sanctify.

Instead, let us continue to proclaim the truths revealed in the Scriptures, even when they contain the difficult dialectic of knowing God as Father without reducing divinity to a human, gendered image. We preach mysterious aspects of God's character best by admitting what we don't understand, continuing to affirm the truths the Bible declares without needing to explain how they are possible, and trusting that God will ultimately be fully revealed and fully known.

We preachers can't explain how God can be three and one, but we proclaim that God is both. As a model, the Athanasian Creed unabashedly professes these truths:

> *This is the catholic faith:*
> *We worship one God in trinity*
>   *and the Trinity in unity,*
>   *neither confusing the persons*
>   *nor dividing the divine being.*
> *For the Father is one person,*
>   *the Son is another,*
>   *and the Spirit is still another.*
> *But the deity of the Father, Son, and Holy Spirit*
>   *is one, equal in glory,*
>   *coeternal in majesty.*
> *What the Father is,*
>   *the Son is,*
>   *and so is the Holy Spirit . . .*
> *Almighty is the Father;*
>   *almighty is the Son;*
>   *almighty is the Spirit;*
> *And yet there are not*

> *three almighty beings,*
> *but one who is almighty . . .*
> And in this Trinity,
> 　*no one is before or after,*
> 　*greater or less than the other;*
> but all three persons are in themselves,
> 　*coeternal and coequal;*
> 　*and so we must worship*
> 　*the Trinity in unity*
> 　*and the one God in three persons.*[11]

Reading the Athanasian Creed periodically (my childhood congregation confessed it together every Trinity Sunday) is good practice for embracing the dialectic of one and three.

GOD'S SOVEREIGNTY AND HUMAN FREE WILL

One dialectical combination is difficult to hold because it sets an attribute of God—that He is sovereignly in control—against the human characteristic of free will. Unless these are suitably balanced we won't respond rightly to the world's evils.

Some theologians say evils exist because God is still in the process of becoming powerful enough to do something about them. But then is God **God?** Dualistic religions instead posit two equally powerful gods, one good and the other evil. But how could we live, never knowing which god is on top today?

Rather, the dialectical tension is not between two gods or within God, but between God and human beings, whom He has endowed with free will so immense that He will not sovereignly override our choice to love and obey Him or not. Preachers need strong theological muscles to keep this dialectic balanced, for to over-accentuate God's sovereignty is to turn human beings into robots without any capacity to resist divine programming and fated to do whatever God's control requires.

To go overboard on the human free will side is to fall into chaos and nihilism. If God is not cosmically supreme, then all hell breaks loose. There is no source of hope for those who suffer.

But God **is** sovereign, and human beings aren't robots because of God's immense desire that we might love Him without coercion. Tragically, we have chosen far too much not to love Him, to go our own way, and thereby to multiply the world's sufferings. All our choices against God's good will lead to tragic revolts and results. We wreak havoc . . .

Yet God is so sovereignly good that He is able to bring good out of our tragic choices—often not immediately, but ultimately. Some dialectical pairs are balanced only over a long period of time, with repeated attention to the opposite poles of the tension.

SOVEREIGNTY AND FREE WILL IN EVIL TIMES

Without that last dialectic in these difficult days of injustices and escalating violence, Christians might passively rely inordinately on God's sovereignty or take too much into their own hands by resorting to human wrath—often neither holy nor loving. How can we preach to form listeners who seek only God's vengeance—never forgetting the depths of our sin and need for repentance? We always need to know God more fully, so that out of the abundance of His character our preaching might contribute to the formation of such attributes as humility, repentance, awe, obedience, adoration, service, submission, and willingness to suffer for the sake of others.

To preach these dialectics that are beyond our understanding requires death to ourselves. One author asserted, "I know that on Sunday mornings either I get out alive or the truth gets out alive. There can be only one survivor."[12] Which survives when you are in the pulpit?

THE PREACHER AND THE COMMUNITY

The dialectic of God's Triune oneness suggests the crucial insight that we can't preach well by ourselves. We need the *perichoresis* of the Trinity as that is lived out in the Christian community. Though each member of the church has different substances, yet we compose one Body in Christ, and the fullness of that bonded community enables us to preach all that the Spirit is telling the Church.

Perhaps one reason (of many!) that many preachers today struggle with low morale is that their community of faith lacks adequate theological muscle for holding various dialectics together. We need all the Body's members to know God's attributes more fully, to hold us in check lest we over-accentuate one side of dialectical pairs, and for appropriate dialectical responses.

Too often congregations split various dialectical sets into two separate camps accentuating one pole or another, and so, for example, we end up with separate "traditional" and "contemporary" services of worship, instead of using the music of the whole Church for the sake of the whole world. Or churches specialize in evangelism or social action without recognizing that the two are dialectically intertwined. We need the whole Body together, with all the members contributing their spiritual strengths to pull the elbows equally well and not split the fullness of the Church's witness to the whole world in word and deed.

PREACHING GOD'S WHOLE CHARACTER SO THAT LISTENERS MIGHT BE WHOLLY FORMED

God's infinitely full character often seems contradictory. Consequently, our preaching of His consummate Being entails constant balancing of such pairs as transcendence and immanence or God's compassion and rebuke. Similarly, we call for various dialectical responses—the tensions of individual faith and common formation or the love of both God and neighbors.

May the sets described in this essay prompt your own reflection on other aspects of your preaching to see whether certain elbows are dominating others, resulting not only in some significant truths inadequately taught but also in misunderstandings of dialectical counterparts. What other aspects of God or human actions and attitudes should be better balanced?

Most important, God's whole character invites us back to the vision we have in Jesus of suffering and eschatological glory, of Christ's transcendence through affliction. Because we know hope through His resurrection, ascension, and the gifts of Pentecost, we are formed with a willingness to carry our cross. Christ's transcendence keeps our suffering from being masochistic, while His suffering keeps our eschatological hope from being triumphalistic.

To preach these truths is to proclaim a God worth believing in, to invite listeners into deep transformation, to change the world.

Notes

1. The media and political worlds have robbed many words of their former weight. See Jacques Ellul, *The Humiliation of the Word,* trans. Joyce Main Hanks (Grand Rapids: William B. Eerdmans Publishing Company, 1985).

2. See George Lindbeck, *The Nature of Doctrine: Religion and Theology in a Postliberal Age* (Philadelphia: Westminster Press, 1984).

3. I use the capitalized word *Church* to signify the ideal as Christ would have His Body be, and uncapitalized *church* or *churches* to name concrete congregations, fallen and seeking-to-be-faithful realities, more or less living out what Church means.

4. Richard Lischer, "Repeat Performance: Making Preaching Come Alive," *Christian Century,* 119, 18 (August 28-September 10, 2002), 24. This article is an excerpt from Richard Lischer, ed., *The Company of Preachers: Wisdom on Preaching, Augustine to the Present* (Grand Rapids: William B. Eerdmans Publishing Company, 2002).

5. See Miroslav Volf, *Exclusion and Embrace: A Theological Exploration of Identity, Otherness, and Reconciliation* (Nashville: Abingdon Press, 1996), esp. 57-98, and Luke Timothy Johnson, *The Real Jesus: The Misguided Quest for the Historical Jesus and the Truth of the Traditional Gospels* (San Francisco: HarperSanFrancisco, 1996).

6. Martin Luther, *Small Catechism: A Handbook of Christian Doctrine* (St. Louis: Concordia Publishing House, 1943), 6.

7. *The Small Catechism by Martin Luther in Contemporary English: A Handbook of Basic Christian Instruction for the Family and the Congregation*, ref. ed. (St. Louis: Concordia Publishing House, 1968), 4.

8. These comments are from Dr. Terence E. Fretheim's lecture, "Reflections on the Wrath of God in the Old Testament," at the American Academy of Religion/Society of Biblical Literature annual meeting in Denver on November 18, 2001. His paper is published in a slightly abbreviated form in *Horizons in Biblical Theology* 24 (2002).

9. It is not possible here to outline the entire development, but for a very helpful overview see John Howard Yoder, *Preface to Theology: Christology and Theological Method* (Grand Rapids: Brazos Press, 2002).

10. This is explored more fully in Marva J. Dawn, *Corrupted Words Reclaimed* (Grand Rapids: Brazos Press, forthcoming).

11. *Lutheran Book of Worship* (Minneapolis: Augsburg Publishing House, 1978), 54.

12. Ben Campbell Johnson and Glenn McDonald, *Imagining a Church in the Spirit: A Task for Mainline Congregations* (Grand Rapids: William B. Eerdmans Publishing Company, 1999), 102.

For Further Reading

Capon, Robert Farrar. *The Foolishness of Preaching: Proclaiming the Gospel Against the Wisdom of the World*. Grand Rapids: William B. Eerdmans Publishing Company, 1998.

Clark, Erskine, ed. *Exilic Preaching: Testimony for Christian Exiles in an Increasingly Hostile Culture*. Harrisburg, Pa.: Trinity Press International, 1998.

Dawn, Marva. *Powers, Weakness, and the Tabernacling of God*. Grand Rapids: William B. Eerdmans Publishing Company, 2001.

———. *Reaching Out Without Dumbing Down: A Theology of Worship for This Urgent Time*. Grand Rapids: William B. Eerdmans Publishing Company, 1995.

———. *A Royal "Waste" of Time: The Splendor of Worshiping God and Being Church for the World*. Grand Rapids: William B. Eerdmans Publishing Company, 1999.

———. *Unfettered Hope: A Call for Faithful Living in an Affluent Society*. Louisville: Westminster John Knox Press, 2003.

Horton, Michael. *A Better Way: Rediscovering the Drama of God-Centered Worship*. Grand Rapids: Baker Books, 2002.

Lischer, Richard, ed. _The Company of Preachers: Wisdom on Preaching, Augustine to the Present_. Grand Rapids: William B. Eerdmans Publishing Company, 2002.

Lischer, Richard. _Open Secrets: A Spiritual Journey Through a Country Church_. New York: Doubleday, 2001.

Willimon, William H., and Richard Lischer, eds. _Concise Encyclopedia of Preaching_. Louisville: Westminster John Knox Press, 1995.

Jana Childers, Ph.D., interim dean of the seminary and professor of homiletics and speech-communication at San Francisco Theological Seminary, is a Presbyterian minister who served congregations in Kansas and New Jersey before joining the seminary faculty. She holds a B.A. from Wheaton College, an M.Div. degree from Princeton Theological Seminary, and a Ph.D. from the Graduate Theological Union in Berkeley, California.

Interests in the arts, spirituality, and worship supplement Jana's "central and great love"—preaching. She has appeared at churches and conferences across the country in the one-woman show *Berries Red* (1987-97), produced the original musical *Push Up the Sky* (1997-99) at the GTU, and is currently working to bring *Aimee!* a play about the life of Aimee Semple McPherson, to the stage. She is the author of *Performing the Word: Preaching as Theatre* (Abingdon Press, 1998), coeditor of *The Abingdon Women's Preaching Annual, Series I,* and editor of a new volume, *Birthing the Sermon: Women Preachers on Creative Process* (Chalice Press, 2001), which was awarded the Religious Communication Association's Book of the Year award.

Jana has appeared several times on *Thirty Good Minutes,* the television program produced by the Chicago Sunday Evening Club, and was recently featured on the Odyssey Channel's *Great Preachers* series.

11

Preaching as Incarnational Act

Jana Childers

❧ NONVERBAL MESSAGES ARE STRONGER THAN VERBAL MESSAGES.
All day long, Sunday in and Sunday out, it is the nonverbals that tell
the story. Stanford University's great scholar, Albert Mehrabian, has
shown that 55 percent of all meaning received in face-to-face communication is attributable to the speaker's body, 38 percent to the tone of
voice, and only 7 percent to word content.[1] The numbers are shocking.
Mehrabian's formula is counterintuitive, to say the least. Yet contemporary theorists not only uphold his findings but have built much of the
field of nonverbal communication around them.

Ultimately, scholars are telling us what good preachers have always
known: when the verbal message and the nonverbal message conflict,
the congregation will believe the nonverbal; if you want the congregation to focus on the word content, stand behind the pulpit; a preacher
has to have both something powerful to say and a powerful way to say it.
Preachers have known for a long time that the body is important. It's just
that we are not always sure what to do about it. Given that more than 90
percent of the communications enterprise depends on the messages the
body sends, you might think public speakers everywhere would be break-
ing down the doors of gymnastics programs, yoga classes, and ballet stu-
dios. This, of course, is hardly the case. Few preachers today come to the
pulpit (or chancel or table) with many resources for enhancing nonverbal skills—and among some of us there is real uneasiness about the physical disciplines preaching involves.

It is the thesis of this essay that a renewed emphasis on the body's
role in preaching could enliven contemporary preaching. Fortunately the
necessary skills and habitus involved in powerful nonverbal communication are eminently learnable. Learning to use the body in preaching is not
nearly as hard as learning to dance or hit a golf ball. A number of skills

are learned quickly, and others represent the kind of lifelong disciplines that any preacher can cultivate, polish, refine, and revisit week by week and year by year. But there is no such thing as someone whose skills cannot be improved. Neither is there anyone who is above improving his or her skills. Incarnational preaching—preaching that maximizes 93 percent of the sermon's message—is both doable and worth doing.

If we Christian preachers believed what we say we believe about the Incarnation, preaching might not be in trouble in the first place. We say we believe that it mattered that the Word, coming into the world, took on human form. We say we believe that in the taking on of human flesh, Jesus Christ redeemed and sanctified human flesh. We say we believe that God's choice to incarnate the Word of God in a human body was not accidental or casual or meaningless. Some of us even say we believe that preaching parallels the Incarnation in process and pattern—that the way the Word of God is embodied in preaching parallels the way it was embodied in Jesus of Nazareth.[2] But that is not how many of us preach. Many of us preach as if God came as a theorem.

Some of us are like the preacher a friend of mine critiqued as being "a stack of books with a head on top." Others are so focused on wordsmithing, they have no energy for anything else. There are some of us who would rather die than move our feet, and others who can't stop. Lots of us struggle to get our eyes up off the page. And these days there are more than a few preachers who just can't bring themselves to "get out of the pulpit" and into the open space of the chancel, though their congregations are begging them to. All of us are, no doubt, communicating—but it may still be that we are falling short of all that Christian preaching can be, because Christian preaching of necessity has to do with human bodies.

Even if Mehrabian were dead wrong and there were some forms of face-to-face communication where the body's role was minimal, Christian preaching could never be one of those forms. Christian preaching proclaims a Word that came in lumpy, sticky, fleshy form—and spoke. Other world religions may understand their "word" to come from sources of other kinds: oracular visions, visits from angels, images in a dream, notes dictated by a mysterious presence, transcriptions made in a trance. But Christian preachers preach a gospel that came walking and talking and living among us. He came storytelling and partying and baby-cuddling. He came sniffly and blistered, discouraged and elated. He didn't just convey somebody's message; He *was* the message. He came as a preacher in human form embodying the Word. Thus it is wholly appropriate that it is through human preachers that the Word's life continues. Embodied preaching may not be unique to Christianity, but it is uniquely important to it.

It is hard to imagine disembodied, or docetic, preaching being effective at any time. But if we were ever going to downplay the importance of the body, this would be the worst possible time to do it. The starkness of Mehrabian's numbers is for those of us who live at the opening of the 21st century, a timely reminder. This is an age when preachers need to make full use of the body. Indeed it may be argued that the body is among the preacher's most important resources for preaching today. In the competition between the screen and the pulpit, the third dimension is our big ace in the hole. Why would we throw it away with both hands? Two-dimensional screens, whether TV, Cinemax, or Jumbo Tron, lack the very thing we possess in spades. The power of eye-to-eye and breath-to-breath communication outlasts, outaffects, and outpersuades all the flash and glam that screens can muster. Who would prefer to experience their gospel through the cool and distancing filters of technology when they could have it with the intimacy of human eye contact. Who would choose glitz when they could have that sweet tug of kinesthetic response one body makes when another three-dimensional body cuts a swath through space—toward them? Incarnational preaching capitalizes on the advantages embodied preachers have—on three-dimensional movement, on the liveness of live contact and all the power they imply.

PREACHING TO RATTLE THE TEACUPS AND WAKE THE DEAD

Even if we could ignore the body's role in preaching, we would be ill advised to do so. The body is a power source. When the preacher's muscle-memory, kinesthetic energy, powers of concentration, vocal patterns, and body rhythms are offered up in the service of the Word, there are few things on heaven or earth that can match the effect. Volcanic, electronic, nuclear power—or their spiritual equivalent—is released. Want to have power, passion, conviction, and authenticity in your preaching? Want your sermons to sail out into the listeners' minds and hearts and not just dribble down the front of the pulpit and out into the aisles? Let your body have its say.

"The body thinks." It was Northwestern University's great scholar Leland Roloff who said it; he taught his oral interpretation classes that the body knows things about interpreting a text the mind cannot know. Only in the process of a careful oral rehearsal of the text can certain things be discovered. "Expression deepens impression," Dr. Roloff claims.[3] Charles Bartow, chair of the speech communication department at Princeton Theological Seminary, agrees. Dr. Bartow gives an example of this principle when he points out how Ps. 27 is often misunderstood by commentators who have not taken the trouble to read it out loud. A number of writers have ventured the opinion that this familiar psalm— which starts, "The LORD is my light and my salvation" (v. 1, RSV) and shifts to "Cast me not off, forsake me not, O God of my salvation!" (v. 9, RSV)—was originally two different psalms. However, when a preacher explores the text through reading it aloud, Dr. Bartow shows, it is easy to discover that the passage contains a classic reversal—the fear that is the subtext of the first half of the psalm becomes the dominant text in the second, and the confidence that is dominant in the first half becomes the subtext in the second.[4] In other words, the body is a storehouse—not only of energy and power but also of wisdom and insight.

Most importantly, it is from the body that preachers derive the ability to concentrate, an ability that undergirds every creative act, from prayer to imaginative thinking. Concentration, like other body-based skills, can be learned and improved, virtually throughout life. In the Church, we are more likely to think of spiritual experience as "opening ourselves to God" or "paying attention to God." "Contemplation" is a word sometimes used for this quality. However the skill of concentration is part and parcel of many spiritual experiences, and as artists have long known, concentration is something that can be developed and improved.

Constantine Stanislavski, perhaps the most famous acting teacher of the 20th century, is reported to have set his students such tasks as memorizing a patterned wallpaper, selecting and following a single sound through a noisy crowd, and solving complex arithmetic problems in their heads. For the preacher there are many small disciplines that can be undertaken on a day-to-day basis to build the concentration "muscle." Many of them can be practiced while waiting in line at the bank or when stuck in traffic. They include, for example,

memorizing Scripture
taking yoga
jogging
singing without looking at the hymnal
contemplative prayer
centering prayer
holding focus on a tune in your head while other music is playing
taking a ballet class
memorizing a visual experience, like a tree

Related to the ability to concentrate is the ability to access the unconscious. If there is any realm of the human psyche where the Holy Spirit seems to delight in playing, moving, and inspiring, it is the unconscious. If there is any source of imagination and generativity in human experience, it is the unconscious. No art, preaching, or creating happens apart from it.

Until recent decades, human creativity was thought of as a willy-nilly thing. Associated since the days of Plato with madness or neurosis, it was often viewed as an impenetrable mystery. Nearly a century ago, theorists began pointing to the unconscious mind as the seat of human creativity. Several decades later, studies began showing the feasibility of "accessing the unconscious"—that is, being able to call upon its imaginative, generative, problem-solving powers. Today creativity theorists speak of achieving a state of "flow," where the artist is optimally challenged, able to maintain peak concentration and access the unconscious for an extended period. Again, there are principles for this kind of work that are easily learned:

• *The unconscious can be trained to kick in.* If a preacher sits down at the same time every day to do his or her creative work, eventually the unconscious will start responding on cue. I had a mentor who told me just before he died at the age of 82 that he "had a 10 A.M. appointment every Tuesday with the Holy Spirit." He had, he said, never been stood up. Other artists have described this discipline as "clearing a space"; focusing and deepening concentration are followed by wading through what best-selling author Anne Lamott calls "the voices."

> You try to quiet your mind so you can hear what that landscape or character has to say above the other voices in your mind. The other voices are banshees and drunken monkeys. They are the voices of anxiety, judgment, doom, guilt. Also, severe hypochondria. There may be a Nurse Ratched-like listing of things that must be done right this moment: foods that must come out of the freezer, appointments that must be canceled or made, hairs that must be tweezed. But you hold an imaginary gun to your head and make yourself stay at the desk.[5]

• *To access the unconscious, still the conscious mind.* Why is it that our best ideas occur in the shower or swimming pool or while we're washing the dishes? Is there something magic about the water? No. It's the large-muscle repetitive movement. It lulls the conscious mind. Pacing, vacuuming, and bicycling also work. When rhythmic movement relaxes us, the activity of the unconscious comes to the fore—or at least it becomes more likely that we will notice such activity.

• *To access the unconscious, eliminate distraction.* Why do we so often have breakthroughs and insights when we're driving, jogging, or walking? Is it the pavement? No it's the lack of distraction. To reach the creativity storehouse of the unconscious, the preacher must eliminate distraction. Distraction is the very definition of what keeps the conscious mind alert. So it is not during a drive through town that the solution to the problem you've been niggling over is likely to occur to you but during a long-distance drive. The closer you are to a trance-like state, the closer you are to a sudden insight. Want to access the unconscious? Eliminate distraction.

• *The unconscious is not interested in sequence.* As Ann Ulanov says, "The Holy Spirit moves in simultaneity, not sequentiality."[6] So it is with the unconscious. Neither works by revealing long chains of cause-and-effect relationships. Neither moves in tidy lines. In neither do thoughts and insights come up in a "first a, then b, then c" sequence. Instead, the unconscious and the Holy Spirit seem to prefer to dump insight in great massive blobs, unsorted. To put it another way, I often tell the seminarians I teach that just because they had a patently spiritual experience during the writing of the sermon, it does not mean they should leave their thoughts on the page just the way they came out of the pen. (Few preachers actually believe that we are taking verbal dictation from the Holy Spirit, but in the excitement and anxiety of the early stages of preaching, some of us act like it.) "The Holy Spirit needs an editor," I try to tell new preachers gently. "That's your job." All preachers need to take what they have accessed or been given and put it in order. The alternative is preaching "stream-of-consciousness sermons"; it's a genre that has been known to have limited appeal.

The Use of Gestures: Some Rules of Thumb

Since the ancient Greeks, elocutionists, rhetoricians, teachers of oral interpretation, forensic coaches, and little old ladies who gave Expression lessons, have all known certain shortcuts. Observations have been made and generalizations developed by teachers down through the years—about the correspondence of certain mannerisms with certain personality types, for example. Whether or not these short cuts should be shared with the student is a question over which teachers have often not agreed. Certainly, an acting coach using a Method approach would not be likely to give a student such information. According to Stanislavsky, it would be essential to let students make their own discoveries. However, there are a number of reasons why a teacher of preachers might share these ancient rules of thumb: they give students a handle on what can seem like an endless sea of choices; they can help nudge preachers out of their comfort zones; and if the student promises never to use them cookbook style, they can be useful heuristic devices. In addition the principles can be learned quickly and are generally well retained.

Among the most helpful of these shortcuts is Leland Powers's.[7] An early 20th-century elocutionist, Powers had a talent for codifying common wisdom. His chart links literary genres with basic interpretive choices—that is, suggestions for what a reader/interpreter should do with his or her eyes, hands, voice, and so on. Powers believed each piece of literature could be understood as having dominantly one appeal—either to head, heart, or gut. Though a passage might contain traces of all three, Powers insisted one would be dominant. For example, the Psalms appeal to the heart, Pauline materials address the head, and the epic Bible stories of which Cecil B. De Mille was so fond have a gut-level appeal. Powers's approach is particularly useful in both the oral interpretation of Scripture and the sermons that are produced by the process.

It is easy to see that it is not only literature that comes in three flavors but the people who read the literature as well. Each interpreter, it may be argued, is dominantly head, heart, or gut oriented. What is hoped is that the interpreter will find within himself or herself the mannerisms that correspond to the genre of literature he or she is reading, tease those mannerisms to the surface, and extend them until there is a match between the text's persona and the reader's. Examples of each of the genres will help clarify:

● *Head-oriented people* speak briskly more often than others, clipping their words. They raise their pitch to create emphasis on certain words. When they pause, it is to get inside the thought and track along with it, even as the words come out of their mouths. They tend to use direct eye contact. Most interestingly of all, head-oriented people have two nonverbal centers: their fingertips and their eyes. They favor nonverbal clusters of behavior that use one or both. Thinking gestures such as making a tent of the fingers and tapping them together, pointing, slicing the air with the fingertips, and putting a fingertip against the mouth while the eyes are squinting in concentration are typical.

● *Gut-oriented people* speak with more punch than others. They use stress or force (but little or no pitch change) to emphasize key words. When they pause, it is because they need to see the scene they are describing unfold on their mental motion picture screen. They use a mix of direct and indirect (looking up, down, or to the side, without withdrawing the face from view) eye contact as they narrate their stories. When it comes to nonverbals, gut-oriented people favor their torsos and their arms. The athlete's "yes!" gesture where the arm is bent at the elbow, extended in front of the body, and brought sharply down is typical.

• *Heart-oriented people* speak with more vowel elongation than others. They stretch the vowels of the words they want to emphasize: "Whaaaat a sweeeet baaaaby," they say. They pause to let their feelings catch up with their words and use more indirect eye contact than other speakers. Their preferred nonverbal behaviors cluster around their palms and cheeks. It is no accident that benedictions, gospel singing, and Pentecostal worship are all open-palmed events—they are all strongly affective experiences. Similarly, the cheeks of the heart-oriented person are always doing something—dimpling, moueing, radiating, pouting.

It is when the reader's natural home base and the text's collide that problems ensue. When a head-oriented preacher reads a heart-oriented text there can be real trouble. Instead of a long lovely "The Loooord is my liiiight and my salvaaaation!" (see Ps. 27:1) the line sounds brusque and matter-of-fact—something an engineer might say. "[Oh God,] give me not up to the will of my adversaries; for . . . they breeeeathe out violence!" (see v. 12, RSV) is said with all the urgency of somebody ordering a big Mac and fries. Similarly, when a head-oriented preacher reads the gut-oriented line "Belshazzar the king made a great feast to a thousand of his lords, and drank wine before the thousand" (Dan. 5:1, KJV) and punctuates it with a quick dainty point of the finger, instead of a big barrel-chested fist-on-the-hip kind of attitude, the effect is less than optimal. Of course when a gut-oriented person has to wade through a typical Pauline word maze, it can be pretty painful too: "For I AM persuaded, that NEITHER death, NOR life, NOR ANGELS, nor PRINCIPALITIES . . ." (Rom. 8:38, KJV). It's a long verse and in the hands of a gut-oriented reader can amount to a lot of shouting.

Most every reader has all three personas residing within him or her. Powers's method offers a way to "work from the outside in" to find and mine the persona appropriate to the text. By trying on mannerisms, the preacher hopes to call up that aspect of his or her own personality that best matches the text. This out-loud exploration of the text leads to discoveries the mind would not make sitting still, leaning over a pool of light on the desk. The goal of this way of experimenting with the text (or manuscript) is twofold: to uncover insights for the creative process and to nurture the kind of kinesthetic awareness that will inform the preaching moment.

One caveat: This approach should never be tacked on at the last minute. It is meant to be a heuristic device—that is, for experimental use in rehearsal only. If the preacher is walking into the pulpit to read the lesson for the day when he or she thinks for the first time "Wait, what genre is this text? What goes with heart oriented?" it is already too late. The technique is meant to help preachers who are not accustomed to thinking with their bodies, not to provide a cheat sheet for lazy ones.

THE USE OF MOVEMENT: SOME RULES OF FOOT

Speaking from behind a large piece of furniture will tend to focus the congregation's attention on the content of what you are saying. Preaching outside the pulpit—standing in the open space of the chancel—will tend to focus the congregation's attention on the relational side of the message—that is, they'll be thinking about how they feel about you. This is an example of a "rule of foot." Knowing the rule makes it possible for the preacher to make a choice based on something more than the congregation's desire for novelty or the preacher's own worries about being appealing. Other similar rules include:

● *Movement works **with** the thought or feeling it expresses.* The preacher's first priority in the rehearsal of movement, as in the use of gestures and other interpretive expressions, is to work from the inside out. (The section above details a way to work *backward,* using outside mannerisms to access inside experience, but its use should be limited to the experimenting that goes on in rehearsal.) Ultimately all performance decisions —movement, gesture, facial expression, vocal inflection, use of pause, and so on—depend on the ability to call up interior experience and express it. Actors call this discipline "internalization" or "truthfulness." You can only express what you experience, they say. It is important to "outer what you inner." Expressions that overreach experience scream "ham" to everybody in the room. Want to avoid the most embarrassing mistake in the world? Want to improve the authenticity of your preaching? Discipline yourself to "outer what you inner" and nothing more.

When applied to movement, this principle means that individual movements will start with the impulse of the thought or feeling they express and end when the impulse ends. If, for example, the preacher is moving toward the congregation saying, "This is the day which the LORD has made; let us rejoice and be glad in it" (Ps. 118:24, RSV), he or she has several options. The movement of the feet can start on "this" and end on "it" or start on "this" and end on "made." Similarly, the movement could start on "let" and end on "it," depending on how the thought is parsed. The goal is to keep the interior experience of wanting-to-say, the saying and the moving working congruently.

- *The feet are the most honest members of the body.* Freud said it (in the sexist language of his day), "A man cannot lie. If he lies with his lips, he will chatter the truth from his fingertips." Speech teachers have their own faintly biblical-sounding way of talking about this phenomenon: "The truth will out," we say. "And it will be the truth about *you.*" Preachers reveal how we feel about what we are saying in our nonverbal behaviors. When we are feeling shy, we hide our hands. When we are angry, we chop the air. And when we are feeling tentative, we have futzy feet. Nervous feet that cannot seem to decide what direction they want to go, but can't stop moving either—feet that make small, continuous, disorganized movements, are expressing a painful but common feeling, "Let me out of here!" It is the preacher's task to harness this nervous energy (sometimes called "race horse energy") and channel it into purposeful movement.

- *Visual interest is as important as vocal interest and is created by the use of levels, angles, and the strategic use of downstage center.* Pacing is the visual equivalent of monotone. It is something preachers do to soothe themselves. It is not something that serves the message. What creates visual interest? The third dimension. You can add it by moving in triangles. Save downstage center (the spot in the middle of the platform on the edge closest to the congregation) for peak moments (beginnings, climaxes, conclusions), and move at 45-degree angles around it.

- *Movement trumps everything.* If the preacher is standing in the open chancel, speaking softly and holding the congregation in the palm of his or her hand, and a choir member seated behind the preacher crosses her legs, it's all over. The spell is broken, the moment lost. The power of movement to attract attention can hardly be overestimated. Put more positively, movement is one of the preacher's greatest tools. Its ability to create suspense makes it nearly invaluable. There is nothing like something unresolved—something that needs to move toward resolution—to hook an audience. Since Aristotle, speakers have relied on this principle—the audience's attention is attracted and held by ambiguity, tensiveness, and disequilibrium. A pause, a couple of steps, a hand suspended in air for a moment—all are just a few examples of the common use of movement to rivet the congregation's focus.

CONCLUSIONS

A good sermon is the result of many confluences: a sacred text meets a preacher, a preacher speaks to a congregation, the Holy Spirit weaves between. The process is infinitely more complex than that simple sentence suggests, of course. Even when we consider only the factors that preachers have some control over, a good sermon is nearly unmappable. Ultimately, spiritual marvel and mystery account for much of a sermon's power. It is good to admit that fact and celebrate it. What we should not do is let words like "mystery" or "spiritual" encourage our tendency to think of preaching in ethereal, ghostly, or disembodied terms. Preaching is something that happens in bodies.

Honing nonverbal communication skills, disciplining the body to be a responsive, expressive instrument, and cultivating a habitus that respects the body's role in preaching may not be the only tasks to which 21st-century preachers are called, but they will go a long way to tapping one of preaching's greatest power sources.

Notes

1. Albert Mehrabian, *Silent Messages: Implicit Communication of Emotions and Attitudes* (Belmont, Calif.: Wadsworth Press, 1971), 43-44.

2. I develop this idea in an essay in the forthcoming book, *The Purpose of Preaching* (St. Louis: Chalice Press).

3. Leland Roloff, *The Perception and Evocation of Literature* (Glenview, Ill.: Scott-Foresman, 1973).

4. Charles L. Bartow, *The Preaching Moment: A Guide to Sermon Delivery* (Nashville: Abingdon, 1980).

5. Anne Lamotte, *Bird by Bird: Some Instructions on Writing and Life* (New York: Pantheon Books, 1994), 7.

6. Ann and Barry Ulanov, *Primary Speech* (Atlanta: John Knox Press, 1982), 104.

7. For a more thorough discussion of Powers's contribution, see Jana Childers, *Performing the Word: Preaching as Theatre* (Nashville: Abingdon, 1998), 88-91.

For Further Reading

Bartow, Charles L. *God's Human Speech: A Practical Theology of Proclamation.* Grand Rapids: Eerdmans Press, 1997.

Bozarth-Campbell, Alla. *The Word's Body: An Incarnational Aesthetic of Interpretation.* Lanham, Md.: University Press of America, 1997.

Childers, Jana. *Performing the Word: Preaching as Theatre.* Nashville: Abingdon, 1998.

———. *Birthing the Sermon: Women Preachers on Creative Process.* St. Louis: Chalice Press, 2001.

Lowry, Eugene. *The Homiletical Plot.* Atlanta: John Knox Press, 1980.

Moeller, Pamela. *A Kinesthetic Homiletic.* Minneapolis: Fortress Press, 1993.

Rice, Charles. *The Embodied Word: Preaching as Art and Liturgy.* Minneapolis: Fortress Press, 1991.

Ward, Richard F. *Speaking of the Holy: The Art of Communication in Preaching.* St. Louis: Chalice Press, 2001.

David Busic is senior pastor of Central Church of the Nazarene in Lenexa, Kansas. He is coeditor of *Preacher's Magazine* and part-time preaching professor at Nazarene Theological Seminary in Kansas City, Missouri.

David and his wife, Christi, have three children, Megan, Benjamin, and Madison.

12

Planning the Preaching Calendar

David Busic

❦ I AM A PASTOR, JUST LIKE YOU. I FACE THE SAME PRESSURE TO preach biblical, relevant sermons to the same people week after week. For the busy pastor, sermons buzz by like telephone poles on the highway—very quickly! With heavy demands on our time, it feels as if Sunday comes every three days. The last thing we need is to wake up every Monday morning and wonder: "What should I preach next Sunday?" How, then, should we decide in advance what to preach?

Deciding what to preach ordinarily occurs in one of two ways: randomly or systematically. Random preaching decisions are usually influenced week in and week out by the preacher's personal intuitions and pastoral observations. Systematic preaching decisions are informed by long-range planning and strategic scheduling of sermon topics. There are arguments against and for a long-range preaching plan.

ARGUMENTS AGAINST A PREACHING PLAN

1. *A sermon planned in advance won't be spontaneous.* After all, how can a sermon planned months in advance possibly anticipate the needs of a congregation today? This way of thinking is not supported by reason or experience. Those who give themselves to advanced planning will be amazed at the timeliness of a sermon prepared even months ahead of time.

2. *A sermon planned in advance won't be relevant to current issues.* What if an event of major importance occurs that dramatically affects the lives of those in my congregation? Fred Craddock points out that a preaching plan is a servant, not a master.[1] The preacher can always adjust the preaching schedule if something previously unknown should take precedence. The Columbine school shooting and the events of 9/11 are obvious examples of important adaptations to the sermon schedule.

3. *A sermon planned in advance will miss what God is trying to say.* The same Holy Spirit who can guide the preacher on what to preach the Monday before the sermon is to be preached, can also guide a preacher well in advance. If God can anoint the preacher's lips when he or she steps to the pulpit, then God can also anoint the preacher's imagination long before the preaching moment. That doesn't take away the need to pay close attention to the promptings of the Holy Spirit in the process. The preacher must always give God permission to interrupt and change plans at any time.

Advantages of a Preaching Plan

1. *Better sermons.* The best sermons are those that grow and mature over a period of time. They are usually "superior homiletically, theologically, and biblically—as well as in ease and freedom of delivery—to those 'gotten up' just days or even hours prior to the presentation."[2]

2. *Less anxiety.* There is tremendous pressure to have to "work up" a sermon every week, especially if no clear need seems to arise. As the week progresses and Sunday looms large, the first temptation is to return to a favorite text or topic that the preacher feels most comfortable with or passionate about. The second temptation is to keep putting off the sermon until later in the week, waiting (and sometimes praying) for some crisis in the world to surface. Many times that crisis isn't precipitated until Saturday night when the preacher is desperate for homiletical inspiration! Our temptation, then, is to locate a great illustration and hope we locate a scripture to match it. A preaching plan gives clear direction before the pressure mounts, offering plenty of time for the preacher's thoughts to come together.

3. *More creativity.* Imagination takes time. The seeds of creativity need time to germinate. A farmer doesn't assume that planting corn on Saturday will give him corn on the cob on Sunday. Planting must precede harvest. Cramming on the farm is no different from cramming for a sermon. Sermon preparation needs time to cultivate embryonic ideas, organize one's thoughts, and consider ways to creatively communicate the message with fresh vitality. Advanced preparation also aids the creativity of those who are planning worship services to complement and enhance the sermon.

Augustine is widely considered to have written the first homiletical textbook.[3] He believed that the threefold purpose of preaching was to teach, delight, and move. Obviously, the "moving" part is God's job. But the "teaching and delighting" parts are the preacher's job. Teaching means communicating the truth of a biblical text in a clear and applicable manner. Delighting simply means interesting. We want our sermons to be engaging and compelling so our people will want to listen. Advanced preparation can only help that creativity.

4. *Available resources.* Many preachers waste a lot of time searching for sermon material. It is frighteningly easy to squander hours snooping around for an engaging story, the perfect illustration, and contemporary analogies. More than a few preachers have let precious sermon preparation fritter away by saying: "I know that story is in one of these files!" But what if the preacher knows what he or she is looking for ahead of time? Then the sermon has time to work in the preacher's mind, and suddenly daily living becomes a homiletical garden[4] of fresh ideas.

I have found it helpful to keep a hanging file drawer of future sermon series close. Then every time I read or observe something remotely connected to the sermon series, I tear out the article, photocopy the book page, or scribble the thought down on a piece of paper and throw it in the appropriate file. Amazingly, when it comes time to flesh out the series and write the sermons, I have a file bulging with ideas. Instead of spending time searching for relevant material, I am weeding out the excess!

5. *Promotes balance.* A preaching plan helps guide the sermon selection process to be a healthier, well-rounded approach. When I am not prepared, I know how easy it is to offer up my favorite dish for the congregation's "Sunday dinner." A comprehensive plan enables me to prepare a square meal every Sunday from every food group in God's Word. I also find myself less prone to personal soapboxes and subjective whims. Otherwise, "pastoral concern for the balanced diet of the parishioners gets lost in the scramble for 'something for Sunday.' But even those trapped in this method know that the cook's appetite for squash does not justify serving it three times every day."[5] I will say more about this in the "Biblical Genres" section of this chapter.

6. *Not reactionary.* A preaching plan becomes a friend of a pastor when dealing with sensitive subjects. Because people know when you address a prickly pear that you aren't shooting from the hip to deal with the most current church hot potato. They know you have had this sermon planned for a long time. On the other hand, "If a preacher has no plan, and no sermon well on the way to maturity, then the slightest noise in the community will sound like a cannon in the homiletically empty ear and the slightest ripple in the congregation will register like an earthquake on that blank paper on the minister's desk."[6] There is great danger in treating issues too quickly before adequate thought or preparation has

been made. Many issues that hit headfirst in the middle of the week would be better handled in personal conversation after time to process.

These are some of the distinct advantages of a preaching plan. How does one go about developing a preaching plan?

A WORKING MODEL FOR DEVELOPING A PREACHING PLAN

When I was called to be the pastor at my current assignment, I made clear with the ministry leaders and congregation that I viewed preaching as one of the most important roles in the plethora of pastoral responsibilities. By making preaching a priority from the very beginning, they graciously agreed to give me two weeks per year to devote to the task of long-range sermon planning. This was not considered vacation or professional development, but intentional times set aside to prayerfully and strategically prepare a comprehensive and holistic plan for preaching.

I usually take four to five days in January and again in July for my study leave. I try to spend that time at a retreat center, instead of a hotel setting, because the cost is less and I find myself less disturbed with other concerns or distracted to watch television. The other advantage of a retreat center is that many have small libraries, prayer rooms, and even cafeterias that are convenient. Access to Internet resources is helpful, but not necessary. I bring several study Bibles, my laptop computer, journal, and pertinent files and books. My time is spent in prayer, reflection, reading, and writing.

I frame my thoughts for a preaching plan around four distinct categories:

Christian Calendar

The first category of my preaching plan is the Christian calendar. The value of the Christian calendar is twofold: (1) it organizes our lives around the major events of our Christian faith; and (2) it enables us to celebrate common time with other Christians around the world. In the Christian calendar, we find that "the Kerygma is proclaimed, [and] the plan of salvation is reviewed in the cycle of the Christian year. The church calendar protects congregations from their preacher's moods and hobbies; its use keeps the choice of what to preach about from being just personal selection."[7]

The seasons of the church year that guide my preaching are Advent/ Christmas, Lent/Easter, and Pentecost. I have chosen not to include

Epiphany as a designated season in my preaching calendar because its major topic of evangelism is a primary emphasis throughout my preaching. The following are just a few of the possible preaching themes and biblical books for preaching from these seasons.

Advent Preaching Themes and Books
Themes: The Incarnation, birth of Christ, God's love, waiting on God's timing, the plan of redemption, and the second coming of Christ
Books: Isaiah, Matthew, Luke, Galatians, Philippians, Colossians, Revelation

Lenten/Easter Themes and Books
Themes: The ministry and passion of Jesus, the Atonement, the Cross, grace, repentance, discipleship, spiritual disciplines, self denial, suffering, the Resurrection, new life, abundant living
Books: Isaiah, Jeremiah, Hosea, the Gospels, Acts, Romans, Philippians, Hebrews

Pentecost Themes and Books
Themes: The Church, evangelism, the person and work of the Holy Spirit, life in the Spirit, holiness
Books: Ezekiel, John, Acts, Pauline and General Epistles

Special Days
Along with these seasons are special days of emphases that merit our preaching focus. These include Ash Wednesday, Maundy Thursday, Good Friday, Trinity Sunday, and Reformation Sunday.

What About the Secular Calendar?

Even though the Christian calendar should have priority over the secular calendar, that does not mean a preacher should ignore other nationally recognized holidays. Mother's Day, Father's Day, Independence Day (or whatever national holiday is recognized by your country), and others can all add significance and relevance to your preaching.

What About the Lectionary?

Some preachers have found great help in following the Christian calendar from the lectionary. The lectionary is a kind of assigned reading list of the central themes of the Christian faith.[8] It leads the church through a three-year cycle of Scripture readings by appointing particular lessons for each Sunday of the year. Usually those texts include an Old Testament reading, a psalm, an epistle, and a Gospel reading. The lectionary is a wonderful tool if for no other reason than it assists in the regular public reading of Scripture in worship.

Getting Started

Because the Christian calendar is the primary framework within which I choose to preach, I am now ready to begin sermon planning. At this point I lay out a blank annual calendar of the coming year and write in the major seasons and holidays. A preaching calendar in the first phase would look something like this:

Example No. 1:
January
February—*Lent (Ash Wednesday)*
March—*Lent*
April—*Lent/Easter (Palm Sunday, Maundy Thursday, Good Friday)*
May—*Easter (Mother's Day)*
June—*Pentecost (Trinity Sunday, Father's Day)*
July—*(Independence Day)*
August
September
October—*(Reformation Sunday)*
November—*(Thanksgiving)*
December—*Advent/Christmas*

Biblical Genres

The second category of my preaching plan is biblical genres. We come across many different forms of communication in our daily experiences. The telephone, fax machine, and E-mail are a few of the ways we communicate. Forms are common in literature as well. Literary forms are called genres, and each genre has a different purpose. There is a difference between an encyclopedia and a poem. There is a difference between a biography and a short story.

Literary genres even contain "forms within the forms." For example, in a newspaper there are headlines and editorials, crossword puzzles and obituaries, box scores and advice columns. Yet these subforms are all part of the form of "newspaper." There are also different forms of letters. There are love letters and memos. There are resignation letters and recommendation letters.

The various forms of literature communicate a particular meaning. One would not interpret the comics in a newspaper the same way one would interpret the stock market report (although in recent days their results are not far apart!). One would not read a "Dear Grandma" letter in the same way one would read a "Dear John" letter. They have different purposes and, therefore, different meanings. Forms are the vehicles that carry our messages to each other. They help us communicate.

The Bible also comes to us in literary forms. God has chosen to communicate with his people through a variety of genres including narratives, letters, poems, prophetic oracles, proverbs, and apocalyptic, just to name a few. In keeping with a literary focus, within these genres are "forms within the forms." Under the category of psalms, we have thanksgiving psalms, lament psalms, creation psalms, and royal psalms.

Why is there such a variety of communication forms in the Bible? Because the plan of redemption cannot be expressed in a single way! Each biblical genre has a particular function to accomplish. They are to do something in the lives of their hearers. The task of the preacher is to discover that function and to prepare the sermon in such a way that the biblical purpose refunctions in the life of the congregation.

We would not preach a lament psalm in quite the same way we would preach a miracle story. Why not? Because they have a different function. We would not preach from Ezekiel the way we would preach from 1 Timothy. Why not? Because a prophetic function is different from a pastoral epistle function. The difference is "not only in what the two texts *say* but also because of *how* the texts say what they say."[9]

All biblical genres attempt to move its audience to action. We are best able to preach biblically if we understand what the intention or function of each passage is. For a sermon to be truly biblical, it must function in similar ways that the passage being preached from intended to function. We need the variety of forms to communicate the whole message of God.

Preaching from Biblical Genres

By including various biblical genres in my preaching plan, I am advocating a well-balanced scriptural diet for my people. It is one thing to feed crackers to someone if it is all you have to offer, but to feed them exclusively crackers when you also have filet mignon and German chocolate cake is another thing. I don't want to simply "feed" my flock my favorite dishes. I want them to feast at the table of the whole counsel of God. That's why I shudder when I hear a pastor say, "I've been preaching from Ephesians for three straight years!" Not only is that congregation malnourished, but they are very likely "fed up" with Ephesians!

I have created a spreadsheet on the books of the Bible that tells me when and what I have preached from each book. In so doing, I am able to track whether or not I have tended to spend an inordinate amount of time preaching from particular books while virtually ignoring others. If in my evaluation of the previous year's preaching calendar I discover that I have preached 27 times from Matthew and not at all from the Minor Prophets, it is an indicator that I may need to consider a series from Malachi. It is my goal to preach from every major biblical genre in a three-year period.

Preaching occasional series from various books of the Bible is an excellent way to offer a balanced diet. I vary my book studies between Old Testament and New Testament for variety. Most of my series are between 7 and 8 weeks long, rarely longer than 12. The summer seems to be a good time for an extended series. If I am preaching on "The Life of David," I may spend 10 weeks in 1 Samuel one year, take a break, and return the next summer to 2 Samuel. Shorter series of 2 to 3 weeks, interspersed between longer series, can also be an effective way of preaching different genres.

A preaching calendar in the second phase might look something like this:

Example No. 2
January—*Genre Series*
February—*Lent (Ash Wednesday)*
March—*Lent*
April—*Lent/Easter (Palm Sunday, Maundy Thursday, Good Friday)*
May—*(Mother's Day)*
June—*Pentecost (Trinity Sunday, Father's Day)*
July—*Genre Series (Independence Day)*
August—*Genre Series*
September
October—*Genre Series (Reformation Sunday)*
November—*(Thanksgiving)*
December—*Advent/Christmas*

Church Vision

The third category of my preaching plan is church vision. Church vision has to do with the direction I believe God wants our family of faith to go in the future. What does God intend for us to do as a local church? What plans, strategies, and dreams need to be communicated through the pulpit ministry?

The preaching for this phase consists of regular, ongoing strategies such as Christian stewardship, financial support of international missions (called Faith Promise in my denomination), preparing for special emphasis weeks (revivals, retreats, etc.), communicating the mission statement and values of our local church, annual "State of the Church" sermons, and clear teaching about particular evangelistic and spiritual growth methodologies unique to our congregation.

Planning for this phase includes preparing for unusual stages in the life of the church or new ministries on the horizon. Our church has recently gone through a capital campaign for a major expansion to our facility. As a way to prepare for that campaign, I preached a series called *Seize the Moment,* which included five messages on the themes of sacrifice, commitment, and Christian stewardship. Our leadership team is also inaugurating a comprehensive, church-wide small-group ministry. To introduce this concept to the congregation, I preached a four-week series called *The Connecting Church,* which emphasized the importance of Christian community in our lives.

Seeker Series

I have also chosen to include as a regular part of my annual preaching plan two "seeker series" per year. These are sermon series designed with the unchurched in mind. They are usually topical in nature and deal with issues that would be both interesting and a felt need in people's lives. While these are "seeker sensitive" sermons, they are not so "seeker driven" that the believers of our church could not benefit from the preaching as well.

Bill Hybels points out some important aspects of this type of series: "With the non-Christian, you want to break the pattern of absenteeism. Over the course of the series, he or she gets in the habit of coming to church and says, 'This isn't so bad; it only takes an hour.' You're trying to show him or her that this is not a painful experience; it's educational and sometimes even a little inspirational. Sometimes it's convicting, but in a thought-provoking rather than heavy-handed way."[10]

We typically prepare touch cards promoting the upcoming series and distribute them to our regular attenders with the encouragement to hand them out to friends and invite them to church. We have discovered that the two times of the year that unchurched people usually consider coming to church are at the close of summer vacation and early spring. For this reason we planned these series for late August/September and the weeks following Easter.

A few of the "seeker series" I have preached are: "Dealing with Feelings: How God Works Through Our Emotions"; "Turning Houses into Homes: God's Design for Healthy Families"; and "Marriage by the Book" with sermon titles such as "Navigating the Communication Highway," "Making the Most of Our Differences," and "Affair-Proofing Your Marriage."

A preaching calendar in the third phase might look something like this:

Example No. 3
January—*Genre Series*
February—*Lent (Ash Wednesday)*
March—*Lent*
April—*Lent/Easter (Palm Sunday, Maundy Thursday, Good Friday)*
May—*Seeker Series (Mother's Day)*
June—*Pentecost (Trinity Sunday, Father's Day)*
July—*Genre Series (Independence Day)/Church Vision*
August—*Genre Series*
September—*Seeker Series*
October—*Genre Series (Reformation Sunday)*
November—*(Thanksgiving)/Church Vision*
December—*Advent/Christmas*

Congregational Cries

The fourth category of my preaching plan is congregational cries. Congregational cries refer to those needs in my congregation that I determine need to be addressed through pastoral preaching. From the beginning of my pastoral ministry, I have kept a pastoral care notebook in which I record every significant encounter with parishioners. This is a loose-leaf binder that contains one sheet for every family unit in my congregation. Every time I have a noteworthy pastoral contact with someone—whether by phone, E-mail, lunch, or home visit—I record the conversation. A journal entry might look something like this:

11/20/02—Met with John for lunch. He is struggling with how to know God's will for his life. Is afraid God may ask him to do something he isn't capable of doing. Encouraged him to trust that God will never lead him to do what He will also not empower him to accomplish.

I bring these notebooks with me on my sermon planning retreats. As I read through them again, it accomplishes three things: (1) it gives me an opportunity to intercede for my flock; (2) it helps me to know if there is a family or individual that I have not had significant contact with in the past year; (3) I prayerfully search for common themes, problems, or questions that may arise in the life of my congregation. If I notice that an inordinate number of people have mentioned struggling to find a meaningful prayer life, it may mean that I need to prepare a message series dealing with prayer. If it becomes obvious that a number of people have lost loved ones, it may mean that I need to prepare a message series dealing with grief and loss.

On one study retreat, I remember how shocked I was to discover how many of our people were battling with some kind of addictive behavior. A large number had family members or were themselves in the grip of something that was controlling their life. From that insight I prepared a series titled "The Habits That Harm Us: Finding Freedom from Life's Hidden Addictions." The topics included dealing with workaholism, substance abuse, codependency, gambling, and sexual addictions. This series was a turning point for many in our church that found victory over habits and a freedom in Christ they had never known before. That might not have happened without the help of a pastoral care notebook as an integral part of my preaching plan.

Preaching as Pastoral Care

As my church has grown in numbers, it has become increasingly clear to me that I cannot personally give sufficient pastoral care to all of my people through one-on-one contacts. But the one way I can give strong pastoral care to large groups of people is through my preaching. Stuart Briscoe has aptly said: "Sitting in my congregation on any given Sunday are a multitude of needs and expectations, levels of maturity and orientations. And I'm supposed to offer a preaching menu to nourish every one of them. That means I've got to be an intentional biblical nutritionist."[11]

A word of caution is in order: Be careful of betraying confidences when preaching from congregational cries. I never use a personal encounter with someone in my church as an illustration in my sermon unless I have his or her permission first. Even then we must be very careful not to embarrass people with the nitty-gritty details of someone's experience. Even if the story is about someone from a previous church, our listeners might wonder if they will be sermon fodder in the future and think twice about talking to us about personal matters.

A preaching calendar in the fourth phase might look something like this:

Example No. 4
January—*Genre Series*
February—*Lent (Ash Wednesday)/ Congregational Cries*

March—*Lent*
April—*Lent/Easter (Palm Sunday, Maundy Thursday, Good Friday)*
May—*Seeker Series (Mother's Day)*
June—*Pentecost (Trinity Sunday, Father's Day)*
July—*Genre Series (Independence Day)/Church Vision*
August—*Genre Series/Congregational Cries*
September—*Seeker Series*
October—*Genre Series (Reformation Sunday)*
November—*(Thanksgiving)/Church Vision*
December—*Advent/Christmas/Congregational Cries*

Mixed Messages

Notice that there are times when the four different preaching categories may overlap. There will be times when Biblical Genre and Congregational Cries go together and accomplish the same purpose. There will be other times when Church Vision fits very nicely with the Christian Calendar theme. One category does not take precedence over another. It is simply one way to be sure that there is a coherent plan with a balanced approach.

So What?

Haddon Robinson states that "all preaching involves a 'so what?'"[12] In other words, preaching that connects with people can never just be informational—it must be transformational. Explaining the intricacies of the Levitical sacrificial system might be interesting, but it will not be preaching unless it offers practical application for the lives of our listeners. For this reason I always write "So What?" on one corner of my preaching calendar to remind me that relevance is important. On the other corner I write the acronym K.I.S.S. (Keep It Simple, Stupid!) to remind me that not everyone in my congregation has a master's degree in theology.

Find a Plan That Fits You

This is not a perfect plan. Nor is it the only plan. The most important thing is that a preacher *has* a plan! God is not a God of chaos and confusion. He is a God of order and peace, who honors those who take preaching seriously enough to plan ahead. With the assortment of ways to develop a preaching plan, and the range of topics to cover, how can a preacher ever say, "I guess it's time to move on. I've run out of things to preach!"

Example No. 4—Annual Sunday Morning Preaching Plan
Sample from the Year 2000[13]

Jan. 2	"Radical Optimists" 1 John 2:28—3:3
Jan. 9	Missionary Guest Speaker

Sermon Series—_Famous Last Words: Letters to Churches Then and Now_

Jan. 16	"FLW: First Love" (Rev. 2:1-7)
Jan. 23	"FLW: Stake Your Life on It!" (Rev. 2:8-11)
Jan. 30	"FLW: No Compromise" (Rev. 2:12-17)
Feb. 6	"FLW: The Gaze of God" (Rev. 2:18-29)
Feb. 13	"FLW: Sleeping in Church" (Rev. 3:1-6)
Feb. 20	"FLW: The Door of Opportunity" (Rev. 3:7-13)
Feb. 28	"FLW: Our No. 1 Spiritual Battle" (Rev. 3:14-22)
Mar. 5	"Eagle Christians" (Isa. 40:28-31)

Lent Begins/Sermon Series—_Cross Examinations_

Mar. 12	"CE: 20/20 Vision" (Mark 10:46-52)
Mar. 19	"CE: Presence Isn't Power" (Mark 5:21-34)
Mar. 26	"CE: Broken and Spilled Out" (Mark 14:1-11)
Apr. 2	"CE: The Covenant Cup" (Mark 14:12-31)
Apr. 9	"CE: Our Crucified God" (Mark 15:16-20)
Apr. 16	Easter Musical (Palm Sunday)
Apr. 23	"CE: Awakenings" (Mark 5:21-24, 35-43, Easter)
Apr. 30	"Until" (Luke 15:1-7, Baptism Service)
May 7	"Stormy Faith" (Heb. 8:6-13)
May 14	"The Forgotten Mother" (Gen. 21:8-20, Mother's Day)
May 21	"Contentment" (Phil. 4:10-13)
May 28	"Remember?" (Exodus 12, Memorial Day)
June 4	Guest Speaker (Personal Vacation)

Pentecost Begins

June 11	Guest Speaker (Personal Vacation)
June 18	Missionary Guest Speaker (Faith Promise)
June 25	"The Other Brother" (Gen. 4:1-16)
July 2	"Strangers" (1 Pet. 1:1-2, 13-21; 2:9-12, Independence Day)
July 9	"Knowing God's Will" (Prov. 3:5-6)
July 16	"Don't Take the Bait!" (James 1:12-16)
July 23	Annual State of the Church Sermon
July 30	"The Lion-Lamb Community" (Isa. 11:1-10)
Aug. 6	"The Courage to Doubt" (Ps. 44)

Seeker Sermon Series—_Dealing with Feelings:_
How God Works Through Our Emotions

Aug. 13	"DWF: Grief" (Ps. 102)
Aug. 20	"DWF: Anger" (Ps. 37)
Aug. 27	"DWF: Fear" (Ps. 55)

Sept. 3   "DWF: Depression" (Ps. 42)
Sept. 10   "DWF: Guilt" (Ps. 32)
Sept. 17   "DWF: Desire" (Ps. 51)
Sept. 24   "DWF: Jealousy" (Ps. 73)
Oct. 1   Central Nazarene Church: Our Strategy for Evangelism

Sermon Series—*Learning from the Life of Abraham*
Oct. 8   "Abraham: The Blessing" (Gen. 12)
Oct. 15   "Abraham: The Decision" (Gen. 13)
Oct. 22   Revival Services—Guest Evangelist
Oct. 29   "Abraham: The Promise" (Gen. 15)
Nov. 5   "Abraham: The Call" (Gen. 17)
Nov. 12   "Abraham: The Test" (Gen. 22)
Nov. 19   "Thanksgiving Hunger" (Matt. 5:6, Thanksgiving)
Nov. 26   "The Mutual Marriage" (Eph. 5:21-33)

Advent Begins/ Sermon Series—*Advent According to John the Baptist*
Dec. 3   "AATJTB: Prepare the Way" (Luke 3:1-6)
Dec. 10   "AATJTB: When Less Is More" (Luke 1:1-15)
Dec. 17   Christmas Musical
Dec. 24   "AATJTB: What's Different?" (Matt. 11:1-6)
Dec. 31   "The Kingdom-Coming Business" (Mark 5:1-20)

Notes

1. Fred Craddock, *Preaching* (Nashville: Abingdon Press, 1985), 103.

2. Ibid., 101.

3. Augustine, *On Christian Teaching* (translation and editing by R. P. H. Green: Oxford Press, 1997).

4. Thomas Long, *The Witness of Preaching* (Nashville: Abingdon Press, 1989), 190.

5. Craddock, *Preaching*, 101.

6. Ibid., 103.

7. George Sweazy, *Preaching the Good News* (Englewood Cliffs, N.J.: Prentice Hall, 1976), 62.

8. Barbara Brown Taylor, *The Seeds of Heaven* (Cincinnati: Forward Movement Publications, 1990), 2.

9. Thomas Long, *Preaching and the Literary Forms of the Bible* (Philadelphia: Fortress Press, 1989), 1.

10. Bill Hybels, *Mastering Contemporary Preaching* (Portland: Multnomah Press, 1989), 34-35.

11. Stuart Briscoe, *Mastering Contemporary Preaching* (Portland: Multnomah Press, 1989), 46.

12. Haddon Robinson, *Mastering Contemporary Preaching* (Portland: Multnomah Press, 1989), 59.

13. From David Busic, *Central Church of the Nazarene*, Lenexa, Kansas.

Conclusion

Robert Leslie Holmes, senior minister of First Presbyterian Church of Pittsburgh, Pennsylvania, relates the encouraging story of an aged preacher whose relatives, on the afternoon of his funeral, found his sermon manuscripts neatly tied and filed away. On top was a card with this question in his handwriting: "Where has the influence gone from these sermons I once preached?" On the back of that card he answered his own question, "Where have last year's rays of sunshine gone, and where are last year's raindrops? They have gone into fruits and grain and vegetables to feed hungry people. Forgotten by most, they did their life-giving work. Their influence lives on, often unidentified. In similar fashion my sermons have given their lives by taking up residence in lives that they make more like Jesus and better fitted for heaven."[1]

Pastor, your preaching is an investment in lives for Christ and His kingdom. And your life, poured into this incalculable endeavor will bear fruit—for this life and for the life to come!

Notes

1. Robert Leslie Holmes, "Restoring Our Passion for Excellence in Preaching," *Preaching,* May/June, 1997, 42.